Student Workbook

for

Public Speaking
A Process Approach
Media Edition

Deanna D. Sellnow
North Dakota State University

THOMSON

™

WADSWORTH

Australia • Canada • Mexico • Singapore • Spain • United Kingdom • United States

Printed in the United States of America
2 3 4 5 6 7 05 04 03

Printer: Patterson Printing Company

0-534-55229-3

For more information about our products,
contact us at:
Thomson Learning Academic Resource Center
1-800-423-0563

For permission to use material from this text,
contact us by:
Phone: 1-800-730-2214
Fax: 1-800-731-2215
Web: http://www.thomsonrights.com

Asia
Thomson Learning
5 Shenton Way #01-01
UIC Building
Singapore 068808

Australia
Nelson Thomson Learning
102 Dodds Street
South Street
South Melbourne, Victoria 3205
Australia

Canada
Nelson Thomson Learning
1120 Birchmount Road
Toronto, Ontario M1K 5G4
Canada

Europe/Middle East/South Africa
Thomson Learning
High Holborn House
50/51 Bedford Row
London WC1R 4LR
United Kingdom

Latin America
Thomson Learning
Seneca, 53
Colonia Polanco
11560 Mexico D.F.
Mexico

Spain
Paraninfo Thomson Learning
Calle/Magallanes, 25
28015 Madrid, Spain

CONTENTS

Chapter Four: PERSUASIVE SPEECHES   141

PREFACE

The materials included in this book are designed to provide you (students) with experiential education opportunities in public speaking fundamentals. I believe that learning is best achieved when students:

a. understand particular theories and concepts;

b. experience those concepts and theories by applying them in actual situations;

c. engage in reflection about their performance; and

d. critique the concepts "in action" as they occur both within the classroom walls and beyond it.

Hence, this book briefly summarizes many of the concepts and theories upon which public speaking fundamentals is grounded (Chapter Two). It also provides experiential learning opportunities for each concept addressed. The book also offers a variety of learning tools to assist you as you prepare and present a variety of public speeches. Finally, instructor critique forms, classmate critique forms, self critique forms, and professional critique forms serve to develop your ability to reflect and think critically about the effectiveness of the communication transactions you experience in a variety of contexts.

I hope you will use this book as a map to guide you on your journey to becoming a more effective public speaker and critic of public communication.

COURSE INFORMATION

This chapter includes a model course syllabus for Public Speaking, four tentative class schedules representing both semester and quarter systems, and two activities. Your instructor may use the course syllabus and schedules provided here, or they may supply their own material. Check with your instructor at the beginning of the term.

COURSE SYLLABUS
Public Speaking Fundamentals

Course Meeting Times: _____

Instructor: _____

Office: _____

Office Hours: _____

Phone: _____

Email Address: _____

Course Goal: The goal of this course is to help students become better communicators. We are concerned with teaching how to speak effectively in public. We also intend to help students understand why some people are more effective and others less effective as public speakers. In short, our goal is to provide both the HOW and the WHY, to help students become better speakers and better consumers of public communication.

Objectives:
1. The student will describe the *communication process*.
2. The student will use research skills to prepare speeches.
3. The student will prepare formal and speaking outlines for public speeches.
4. The student will demonstrate effective use of voice and body to deliver public speeches.
5. The student will practice effective listening skills.
6. The student will complete written critiques of public speakers.

7. The student will recognize and understand public speaking terminology.

8. The student will practice techniques to reduce anxiety and increase public speaking proficiency.

9. The student will understand the need for effective oral communication skills in professional and personal settings.

Academic Dishonesty/Plagiarism: Students are expected to turn in original work and present original speeches. Students are also expected to cite (both orally and in writing) ideas drawn from external sources. Students who are caught cheating may be failed for a particular assignment, test, or course based upon the discretion of the instructor.

Required Textbooks and Materials:

Sellnow, D. (2003). *Public Speaking: A Process Approach, Media Edition.*

Sellnow, D. (2003). *Student Workbook for Public Speaking: A Process Approach, Media Edition*

Portfolio folder
3 x 5 inch index cards
Floppy Disk

REQUIRED SPEECHES
(Students must complete all of these speeches during the semester or they will receive a grade of "incomplete" for the entire course):

1. The Speech of Self-Introduction (10 points)*
This is a 2- to 3-minute speech introducing yourself to the class. The lectern is not allowed for this speech. An extemporaneous delivery style (key word outline) is required. You are to speak from a *speaking outline* using no more than two 3 x 5 inch index cards (one side only).

*Problem-based learning approach: After the Self-Introduction speeches, students form four-member groups based on a public problem or issue they would like to study in more detail. These four-member groups will work together to prepare different speeches on the problem or issue throughout the quarter or semester.

2. Informative Speech #1 (42 Points) (a, b, or c below)
(a) The Speech of Personal Significance*
This is a 4- to 6-minute informative speech describing an object, person, event, or belief that has personal significance to you (helped to shape who you are today). Main points should be specific values or beliefs you uphold. Supporting material should come from personal life experiences. Listeners should come away knowing *why* this person, object, event, or belief is important to you. The lectern is not allowed for this speech. Points will be deducted for going over or under the time limits, for not using a *speaking outline* (key words and phrases), or for using more than five 3 x 5 inch index cards (one side only).

*Problem-based learning approach: Students must talk about a public problem or social issue that has personal significance to them.

(b) The Speech of Demonstration
This is a 4- to 6-minute informative speech clarifying a process or procedure in the minds of your listeners. Main points should be arranged chronologically as steps in a sequence. Supporting material

should include definitions, explanations, and examples. Listeners should come away knowing how a process or procedure works. The lectern is not allowed for this speech. Points will be deducted for going over or under the time limits, for not using a *speaking outline* (key words and phrases), or for using more than five 3 x 5 inch index cards (one side only).

(c) The Speech of Narration

This is a 4- to 6-minute informative speech sharing an interesting, entertaining, or inspirational story. This may be about an event that shaped your life or something you heard or read about. It should be designed to illustrate a moral. Supporting material should include personal experiences (your own or from those individuals in your story), examples, and explanations. Listeners should come away knowing the moral of the story. The lectern is not allowed for this speech. Points will be deducted for going over or under the time limits, for not using a *speaking outline* (key words and phrases), or for using more than five 3 x 5 inch index cards (one side only).

3. Informative Speech #2 (with presentational aid) (49 points)
(a or b below)
(a) The Speech of Information and Diversity*

This is a 4- to 6-minute informative speech that uses at least two presentational aids, or one that is used in three different ways. The specific purpose of this speech must take a multicultural perspective. You may elect to compare and/or contrast an aspect of two cultural groups or discuss an aspect of one cultural group in detail. You must step outside of your own cultural perspective in some way. Listener relevance must be included for each main point of the speech. Lectern is not allowed. You must cite at least four external sources during this speech. Points will again be deducted for going over or under the time limits, for not using a *speaking outline* (key words and phrases), or for using more than five 3 x 5 inch index cards (one side only).

Problem-based learning approach: Students must talk about the public problem or social issue they discussed in the speech of personal significance. This time, however, they talk about the relationship between the public problem or social issue as it relates to some cultural group to which they do not belong.

(b) The Speech of Definition

This is a 4- to 6-minute informative speech that uses at least two presentational aids, or one that is used in three different ways. The specific purpose of this speech is to reduce ambiguity by illustrating how one term or concept can be defined in many different ways. Your ultimate goal is to make an abstract concept more concrete for your listeners. The term or concept you select might come from a language other than English. Your supporting material should include both denotative and connotative definitions as well as examples and explanations. Listener relevance must be included for each main point of the speech. The lectern is not allowed. You must cite at least four external sources for this speech. Points will be deducted for going over or under the time limits, for not using a speaking outline (key words and phrases), or for using more than five 3 x 5 inch index cards (one side only).

4. Dispositional Persuasive Speech (42 points) (a or b below)
(a) The Speech of Point-Counterpoint*

This is a 4- to 6-minute dispositional persuasive speech. In other words, you must attempt to form, reform, or reinforce listeners' attitudes or beliefs about an issue. It may focus on a question of fact or a question of value. You and a partner will research and prepare two different speeches advocating opposite sides of the same issue. Although speakers will research and prepare your speeches together to ensure a "clash," speakers will be *graded individually* for your oral presentations. Each speaker must cite at least four external sources during this speech. Lectern and presentational aids are optional for this speech. Points will again be deducted for going over or under the time limits, for not using a *speaking outline* (key words and phrases), or for using more than five 3 x 5 inch index cards (one side only).

Problem-based learning approach: Each dyad selects an opposing argument about the public problem or issue their group is focusing on. Each member of the dyad presents an individual speech on their side of the problem. They might look at two different possible causes for the problem or two different ways to solve it. Or they might consider whether or not the current practices for dealing with the problem are (a) fair, or (b) ethical, or (c) moral, and so on.

(b) The Editorial Rebuttal

This is a 4- to 6-minute dispositional persuasive speech. In other words, you must attempt to form, reform, or reinforce listeners' attitudes or beliefs about an issue. It may focus on a question of fact or a question of value. You will refute the position of someone with whose opinion you disagree. Your speech will refute an editorial you have read in a newspaper. You must cite at least four external sources during this speech. Lectern and presentational aids are optional for this speech. Points will again be deducted for going over or under the time limits, for not using a *speaking outline* (key words and phrases), or for using more than five 3 x 5 inch index cards (one side only).

5. Actuation Persuasive Speech (49 points) (a or b below)

(a) The Actuation Persuasive Symposium*

This is a 15- to 20-minute actuation persuasive speech presented in a group symposium format (4 students per group). In this speech focused on a question of policy, you must attempt to motivate listeners to *act* or to change their *behavior* in some way. Your group may structure the speech using a problem-cause-solution format or using a modified comparative advantages approach or using Monroe's motivated sequence. Three speakers will each prepare and present a 4- to 5-minute minute speech focused on one aspect of the topic using at least two outside sources. One speaker will serve as moderator, providing the introduction, conclusion, and transitions between speakers. The moderator will also type the formal group outline. This speech also requires the use of PowerPoint visual aids *by each presenter.* These visual aids must adhere to the same guidelines as other presentational aids. Lectern is required for this speech. Each speaker will earn both an individual grade (28 points) and a group grade (21 points). Part of the group grade will be based on the Group Dynamics Peer Critique Forms completed by the other members of the group.

Problem-based learning approach: Groups will prepare their symposium speech on the public problem or social issue they have been researching throughout the semester. In their symposium presentation, they will identify and define the problem, clarify its causes, offer potential solutions, identify the best solution, and call their listeners to action.

(b) The Actuation Persuasive Speech by an Individual

This is an 8- to 10-minute actuation persuasive speech. In this speech focused on a question of policy, you must attempt to motivate listeners to act or to change their behavior in some way. You might address a global problem, national problem, local problem, or campus problem. Your thesis statement is formulated around a question of policy. You will use one of four organizational formats for this speech. These formats are: Problem/Solution, Problem–Cause–Solution, Modified Comparative Advantages, or Monroe's Motivated Sequence. You must cite at least six external sources during this speech. Lectern is required for this speech as is the use of PowerPoint presentational aids. Points will be deducted for going over or under the time limits, for not using a *speaking outline*, or for using more than five 3 x 5 inch index cards (one side only).

6. The Impromptu Speech (10 points)
This is a 2- to 3-minute speech, which is prepared in approximately two minutes. You are required to present at least one impromptu speech as your final presentation (during finals week). Your instructor will provide the topic. Lectern is optional for this speech. You are to use a *speaking outline* for this presentation.

EXAMINATIONS (150 points)
Two tests (75 points each) comprised of multiple choice, true/false, matching, or short answer questions will be administered during the semester. Each test covers a portion of the material presented in the textbook, workbook, and class discussions.

SPEECH OUTLINES (46 points)
You are required to turn in a *speaking outline* for each of the six required speeches. You are required to turn in a typed formal outline as well as a preparation outline for speeches #2, #3, #4, and #5.

Typed Formal Outlines: 5 points each (20 points)
Preparation Outlines: 2 points each (8 points)
Speaking Outlines: 3 points each (18 points)

PEER CRITIQUES

1. Classmate Speech Critiques (5 points each)
You will critique a classmate on each speaking day when you are not assigned to speak. These critiques cannot be made up.

2. Group Dynamics Peer Critiques (5 points)
You will complete a group dynamics peer critique for each member of your group, documenting their responsible (or irresponsible) membership in the group. These will be seen only by you and by the instructor.

3. Self Critiques (5 points each)
You will complete a self-critique evaluating your presentation after completing each speech.

4. Reflective Thinking Process Papers (5 points each)
If you are required to complete the actuation persuasive group symposium speech, you will be required to complete process papers detailing the progress of your group while preparing.

5. Professional Speaker Critique (10 points)
You will complete a 1- to 2-page typed critique of a professional speaker who you observe in the community. This person cannot be an instructor in a course. It must be a live performance of a legitimate professional speaker. Verify the appropriateness of your choice with the instructor. You will attach the typed critique to your Audience Assessment form and Professional Speaker Critique notes.

IN-CLASS ACTIVITIES
Your instructor may require in-class activities throughout the semester. Points for these activities may not be made up.

GRADING
90% = A   80% = B   70% = C   60% = D   50% and below = F

6

LATE SPEECH POLICY

Your public speech presentation days will be assigned during the first two weeks of the semester. You must speak on your assigned speaking day or are responsible for "trading" days with a classmate. It is your responsibility to make the trade and to notify the instructor to receive full points. Students who do NOT speak on their assigned day will be evaluated as follows:

a. An Excused Absence: Zero Point Deduction

Students may present their speech with no points deducted during the next class period where time is available for:

(1) A university-sanctioned activity where prior notice has been provided (i.e., sports, music tour, etc.)
(2) Illness verified in writing by a doctor
(3) An emergency with documentation provided through their advisor or the Vice President of Student Academic Affairs

b. Late Speech: One letter grade deduction

Students may present their speech with a letter grade deduction during the next class period where time is available if they provide a compelling excuse. "Compelling" excuses are based on the instructor's discretion. Students MUST notify their instructor prior to their assigned speaking day/time to be considered for this option.

c. Unexcused Absence: Zero points

Students who do not provide an acceptable reason for not giving their speech will make up the assignment at the instructor's discretion for zero points. Unexcused absences include: missing class to study for a test, oversleeping, not being ready to speak, and having to work.

SPECIAL NEEDS

Any students who need special accommodations for learning or who have special needs are invited to share these concerns or requests with the instructor as soon as possible.

Tentative Daily Schedule
Public Speaking Fundamentals
MWF 15-Week Semester Plan

DATE	TOPIC	DUE TODAY
DAY 1	Introduction and Orientation, Why Study Public Speaking?	SW (Syllabus) Daily Schedule SW (Autograph party) SW (Info. Sheet)
	READ: Chapter 1	
DAY 2	Communication Models Ethics in Public Speaking **READ:** Chapter 2 **ASSIGN:** SW (PRPSA)	
DAY 3	Public Speaking Anxiety **READ:** Chapter 3 **ASSIGN:** SW (Informative Self-Introduction Speech)	SW (PRPSA)
DAY 4	Self-Introduction Speeches	SW (prep outline)
DAY 5	Self-Introduction Speeches	SW (evaluation form) SW (self-critique)
	READ: Chapter 4	
DAY 6	Listening and Critiquing **READ:** Chapter 5 **ASSIGN:** SW (Professional Speaking Critique)	
DAY 7	Topic Selection **READ:** Chapter 6 **ASSIGN:** SW (Learning Style Inventory)	
DAY 8	Audience Analysis and the Learning Cycle **READ:** Chapters 7–8 **ASSIGN:** SW (Using the Library)	
DAY 9	Gathering and Citing Supporting Material **READ:** Chapters 8–10	SW (Using the Library)

DAY 10   Organizing & Outlining
                (Macrostructure)
                READ: Chapter 11
                ASSIGN: SW (Informative Speech #1)
                Preparation Outline for Next Time

DAY 11   Language Choices (Microstructure)   SW Preparation Outline
                READ: Chapter 12

DAY 12   Delivery (Use of Voice and Use of Body)
                ASSIGN: Formal Outline for Informative Speech #1

DAY 13   In-class rehearsal day   Formal & Speaking Outlines

DAY 14   Informative Speech #1   SW (Evaluation form)

DAY 15   Informative Speech #1   SW (Classmate Critique)

DAY 16   Informative Speech #1   SW (Self-Critique)

DAY 17   Informative Speech #1

DAY 18   **EXAM #1**   Chapters 1–12
                READ: Chapter 13

DAY 19   Go Over Exam and Presentational Aids
                READ: Chapter 14
                ASSIGN: SW (Informative Speech with Presentational Aid)

DAY 20   Informative Speaking, Cultural Diversity
                ASSIGN: SW (Preparation Outline)
                As well as Formal and Speaking Outlines

DAY 21   In-class rehearsal day   SW (Preparation Outline)
                                                        Formal Outline
                                                        Speaking Outline

| **DAY 22** | Informative Speech w/Aids | SW (Evaluation Form) |

| **DAY 23** | Informative Speech w/Aids | SW (Classmate Critique) |

| **DAY 24** | Informative Speech w/Aids | SW (Self Critique) |

DAY 25   Informative Speech w/Aids
             READ: Chapter 15

DAY 26   Persuasive Speaking: Types and Designs
             READ: Chapter 16
             ASSIGN: SW (Dispositional Persuasive Speech)

DAY 27   Persuasive Speaking: Types and Designs (cont.)

DAY 28   Persuasive Speaking: Rhetorical Strategies
             ASSIGN: Dyads (if doing Point/Counterpoint Speeches)

DAY 29   Work Session
             ASSIGN: (Preparation Outline),
             as well as formal and speaking outlines

DAY 30   In-class Rehearsal Day   Preparation, Formal, and
                                             Speaking Outlines

DAY 31   Persuasive Point Counterpoint Speeches   SW (Evaluation Form)

DAY 32   Persuasive Point Counterpoint Speeches   SW (Classmate Critique)

DAY 33   Persuasive Point Counterpoint Speeches

DAY 34   Persuasive Point Counterpoint Speeches   SW (Self-Critique)
             READ: Chapter 18   SW (Listener Reflection)

DAY 35   Working and Speaking in Groups
             ASSIGN: SW (Actuation Persuasive Symposium Speech)

DAY 36	Work Session ASSIGN: SW (Reflective Paper #1) (Reflective Thinking Process Paper #1 if doing symposium)	
DAY 37	Work Session **ASSIGN:** (Reflective Paper #2) and Bring IBM-formatted disk to class	SW (Reflective Paper #1)
DAY 38	Creating and Using PowerPoint Presentational Aids	SW (Reflective Paper #2)
DAY 39	Work Session **ASSIGN:** (Reflective Paper #3) **READ:** Chapter 17 and SW (Impromptu Speeches)	
DAY 40	Speaking on Special Occasions Impromptu Speaking	SW (Reflective Paper #3)
DAY 41	Impromptu Speeches	
DAY 42	Impromptu Speeches	
DAY 43	**Exam #2** (Chapters 13–18)	SW (Professional Speaker Critique)
DAY 44	In-class rehearsal day (with PowerPoint)	
FINALS:	**Actuation Persuasive Speeches**	SW (Evaluation form) SW (Peer Critique) SW (Self Critique) Individual and Group Formal and Speaking Outlines

Tentative Daily Schedule
Public Speaking Fundamentals
T & Th 15-Week Semester Plan

DATE	TOPIC	DUE TODAY
DAY 1	Introduction and Orientation, Why Study Public Speaking?	SW: (Syllabus) Daily Schedule SW: (ice breaker) SW: (Info. Sheet)
	READ: Chapters 1 and 2 **ASSIGN:** SW (PRPSA)	
DAY 2	Communication Models, Public Speaking Anxiety, Ethics in Public Speaking **READ:** Chapter 3 **ASSIGN:** SW (Informative Self-Introduction Speech)	SW (PRPSA)
DAY 3	Self-Introduction Speeches **READ:** Chapter 4	SW: (prep outline) SW: (evaluation form) SW: (self-critique)
DAY 4	Listening and Critiquing **READ:** Chapters 5 and 6 **ASSIGN:** SW (Professional Speaking Critique) And SW (Learning Style Inventory)	
DAY 5	Topic Selection, Audience Analysis, and the Learning Cycle **READ:** Chapters 7–10 **ASSIGN:** SW (Using the Library)	SW: (Learning Style Inventory)
DAY 6	Structuring, Supporting, & Outlining (Macrostructure) **READ:** Chapter 11 **ASSIGN:** SW (Informative Speech of Personal Significance) Preparation Outline for Next Time (SW)	SW (Using the Library)
DAY 7	Language Choices (Microstructure) **READ:** Chapter 12	SW (Preparation Outline)

12

DAY 8	Delivery (Use of voice and Use of Body) **ASSIGN:** Formal Outline for Informative Speech of Personal Significance	
DAY 9	In-class rehearsal day	Formal & Speaking Outlines
DAY 10	Informative Speech of Personal Significance	SW (Evaluation form)
DAY 11	Informative Speech of Personal Significance	SW (Classmate Critique) SW (Self-Critique)
DAY 12	**EXAM #1** **READ:** Chapter 13	Chapters 1–12 & SW
DAY 13	Go Over Exam and Presentational Aids **READ:** Chapter 14 **ASSIGN:** SW (Informative Speech of Diversity with Presentational Aid)	
DAY 14	Informative Speaking, Cultural Diversity **ASSIGN:** SW (Preparation Outline), As well as formal and Speaking Outlines	
DAY 15	In-class rehearsal day	SW (Preparation Outline) Formal Outline Speaking Outline
DAY 16	Informative Speech of Diversity with Presentation Aids	SW (Evaluation Form)
DAY 17	Informative Speech of Diversity with Presentation Aids	SW (Classmate Critique)
DAY 18	Informative Speech of Diversity with Presentation Aids **READ:** Chapter 15	SW (Self Critique)
DAY 19	Persuasive Speaking: Types and Designs **READ:** Chapter 16 **ASSIGN:** SW (Persuasive Point-Counterpoint Speech)	

DAY 20	Persuasive Speaking: Rhetorical Strategies **ASSIGN:** Dyads for Point/Counterpoint Speeches	
DAY 21	Dyad Work Session **ASSIGN:** SW (Preparation Outline), as Well as formal and speaking outlines	
DAY 22	Persuasive Point Counterpoint Speeches	SW (Evaluation Form)
DAY 23	Persuasive Point Counterpoint Speeches **READ:** Chapter 18	SW (Classmate Critique) SW (Self-Critique) SW (Listener Reflection) Preparation, formal, and Speaking Outlines
DAY 24	Working and Speaking in Groups **ASSIGN:** SW (Actuation Persuasive Symposium Speech)	
DAY 25	Group Work Session **ASSIGN:** SW (Reflective Thinking Process Paper #1)	
DAY 26	Group Work Session **ASSIGN:** SW (Paper #2) and Bring IBM-formatted disk to class	SW (Reflection Paper #1)
DAY 27	Creating and Using PowerPoint Presentational Aids **ASSIGN:** SW (Reflection Paper #3) **READ:** Chapter 17 and SW (Impromptu Speeches)	SW (Reflection Paper #2)
DAY 28	Speaking on Special Occasions Impromptu Speaking	SW (Reflection Paper #3) IMPROMPTU SPEECHES
DAY 29	**Exam #2** (Chapters 13–18 and SW)	SW (Professional Speaker Critique)
DAY 30	In-class rehearsal day (with PowerPoint)	

FINALS: Actuation Persuasive Symposium Speeches

SW (Evaluation form)
SW (Peer Critique)
SW (Self Critique)
Individual and Group
Formal and Speaking
Outlines

Tentative Daily Schedule
Public Speaking Fundamentals
MWF 10-Week Quarter Plan

DATE	TOPIC	DUE TODAY
DAY 1	Introduction and Orientation, Why Study Public Speaking? **READ:** Chapter 1	SW (Syllabus) Daily Schedule SW (ice breaker) SW (Info. Sheet)
DAY 2	Communication Models Ethics in Public Speaking **READ:** Chapter 2 **ASSIGN:** SW (PRPSA)	
DAY 3	Public Speaking Anxiety **READ:** Chapter 3 **ASSIGN:** SW (Informative Self-Introduction Speech)	SW (PRPSA)
DAY 4	Self-Introduction Speeches	SW (prep outline)
DAY 5	Self-Introduction Speeches **READ:** Chapter 4	SW (evaluation form) SW (self-critique)
DAY 6	Listening and Critiquing **READ:** Chapters 5 and 6 **ASSIGN:** SW (Professional Speaking Critique) and SW (Learning Style Inventory)	
DAY 7	Topic Selection, Audience Analysis and the Learning Cycle **READ:** Chapters 7–8 **ASSIGN:** SW (Using the Library)	SW (Learning Style Inventory)
DAY 8	Gathering and Citing Supporting Material **READ:** Chapters 8–10	SW (Using the Library)

DAY 9	Organizing & Outlining (Macrostructure) **READ:** Chapter 11 **ASSIGN:** SW (Informative Speech of Personal Significance) Preparation Outline for Next Time (SW)	
DAY 10	Language Choices (Microstructure) **READ:** Chapter 12	SW (Preparation Outline)
DAY 11	Delivery (Use of Voice and Use of Body) **ASSIGN:** Formal & Speaking Outlines for Informative Speech of Personal Significance	
DAY 12	Informative Speech of Personal Significance	SW (Evaluation form)
DAY 13	Informative Speech of Personal Significance	SW (Classmate Critique)
DAY 14	Informative Speech of Personal Significance	SW (Self-Critique) Formal & Speaking Outlines
DAY 15	**EXAM #1** **READ:** Chapter 13	Chapters 1–12 & SW
DAY 16	Go Over Exam and Presentational Aids **READ:** Chapter 14 **ASSIGN:** SW (Informative Speech of Diversity with Presentational Aid)	
DAY 17	Informative Speaking, Cultural Diversity **ASSIGN:** SW (Preparation Outline), As well as formal and Speaking Outlines	
DAY 18	Informative Speech w/Aids	SW (Evaluation Form)
DAY 19	Informative Speech w/Aids	SW (Classmate Critique)
DAY 20	Informative Speech w/Aids **READ:** Chapter 15	SW (Self Critique) Preparation, formal, and speaking outlines

DAY 21   Persuasive Speaking: Types and Designs
READ: Chapter 16

DAY 22   Persuasive Speaking: Rhetorical Strategies
READ: Chapter 18

DAY 23   Working and Speaking in Groups
ASSIGN: SW (Actuation Persuasive
Symposium Speech)

DAY 24   Group Work Session
ASSIGN: SW (Reflective Thinking
Process Paper #1)

DAY 25   Group Work Session   SW (Reflection Paper #1)
ASSIGN: SW (Paper #2) and
Bring IBM-formatted disk to class

DAY 26   Creating and Using PowerPoint   SW (Reflection Paper #2)
Presentational Aids
ASSIGN: SW (Reflection Paper #3)
READ: Chapter 17 and SW (Impromptu Speeches)

DAY 27   Speaking on Special Occasions   SW (Reflection Paper #3)
Impromptu Speaking

DAY 28   Impromptu Speeches

DAY 29   **Exam #2** (Chapters 13–18 and SW)   SW (Professional
Speaker Critique)

DAY 30   In-class rehearsal day (with PowerPoint)

FINALS: **Actuation Persuasive Symposium Speeches**   SW (Evaluation form)
SW (Peer Critique)
SW (Self Critique)
Individual and Group
Formal and Speaking
Outlines

Tentative Daily Schedule
Public Speaking Fundamentals
T & Th 10-Week Quarter Plan

DATE	TOPIC	DUE TODAY
DAY 1	Introduction and Orientation, Why Study Public Speaking? **READ:** Chapters 1 and 2 **ASSIGN:** SW (PRPSA)	SW (Syllabus) Daily Schedule SW (ice breaker) SW (Info. Sheet)
DAY 2	Communication Models, Public Speaking Anxiety, Ethics in Public Speaking **READ:** Chapter 3 **ASSIGN:** SW (Informative Self-Introduction Speech)	SW (PRPSA)
DAY 3	Self-Introduction Speeches **READ:** Chapter 4	SW (prep outline) SW (evaluation form) SW (self-critique)
DAY 4	Listening and Critiquing **READ:** Chapters 5 and 6 **ASSIGN:** SW (Professional Speaking Critique) And SW (Learning Style Inventory)	
DAY 5	Topic Selection, Audience Analysis, and the Learning Cycle **READ:** Chapters 7–10 **ASSIGN:** SW (Using the Library)	SW (Learning Style Inventory)
DAY 6	Structuring, Supporting, & Outlining (Macrostructure) **READ:** Chapter 11 **ASSIGN:** SW (Informative Speech of Personal Significance) Preparation Outline for Next Time (SW)	SW (Using the Library)
DAY 7	Language Choices (Microstructure) **READ:** Chapter 12	SW (Preparation Outline)
DAY 8	Delivery (Use of Voice and Use of Body) **ASSIGN:** Formal Outline for Informative Speech of Personal Significance	

DAY 9	Informative Speech of Personal Significance	SW (Evaluation form)
DAY 10	Informative Speech of Personal Significance	SW (Classmate Critique) SW (Self-Critique) Formal and Speaking Outlines
DAY 11	**EXAM #1** **READ:** Chapters 13 and 14	Chapters 1–12 and SW
DAY 12	Go Over Exam, Informative Speaking and Presentational Aids **ASSIGN:** SW (Preparation Outline) (Informative Speech with Presentational Aid)	
DAY 13	In-class rehearsal	SW (Preparation Outline)
DAY 14	Informative Speech w/ Aid	Formal Outline
DAY 15	Informative Speech w/Aid **READ:** Chapters 15 and 16	Speaking Outline SW (Evaluation Form) SW (Classmate Critique) SW (Self Critique)
DAY 16	Persuasive Speaking: Types and Designs, Rhetorical Strategies **READ:** Chapter 16 **READ:** Chapter 18	
DAY 17	Working and Speaking in Groups **ASSIGN:** SW (Actuation Persuasive Symposium Speech)	
DAY 18	Group Work Session **ASSIGN:** SW (Reflective Thinking Process Paper #1)	
DAY 19	Group Work Session/PowerPoint **ASSIGN:** SW (Reflection Paper #2) **READ:** Chapter 17 and SW (Impromptu Speeches)	SW (Reflection Paper #1)

DAY 20	Speaking on Special Occasions Impromptu Speaking	SW (Reflection Paper #2) IMPROMPTU SPEECHES
DAY 21	**Exam #2** (Chapters 13–18 and SW)	SW (Professional Speaker Critique)
FINALS:	Actuation Persuasive Symposium Speeches	SW (Evaluation form) SW (Peer Critique) SW (Self Critique) Individual and Group Formal and Speaking Outlines

Name _____

AUTOGRAPH PARTY

Goal: This activity is designed to help you get to know your classmates.

Rationale: One of the primary reasons people experience public speaking anxiety is because they have a "fear of the unknown." Part of this fear stems from the fact that their audience is made up of strangers. One way to reduce this fear and, consequently, reduce the anxiety that stems from it, is to engage in activities that acquaint speakers with their listeners before they actually present a formal speech.

Directions: Try to find a classmate who fits each description below. Have the classmate sign this sheet next to the appropriate description. You must find a *different* person for each description. Each person may sign only one line.

FIND SOMEONE WHO

... is an only child. _____

... skipped breakfast today. _____

... drives a foreign car. _____

... was born east of the Mississippi River. _____

... isn't getting enough sleep. _____

... plays a musical instrument. _____

... was born in July. _____

... is a parent. _____

... is left-handed. _____

... engages in aerobic activity. _____

... has an unusual hobby. _____

... is married. _____

... knows someone whom you know. _____

... has schedule problems. _____

... writes poetry. _____

... has travelled overseas. _____

... is in love. _____

... speaks a language besides English. _____

... has the same major as you. _____

... has eaten liver and onions. _____

STUDENT PERSONAL INFORMATION FORM

Goal: This form will help the instructor get to know you better.

Rationale: Public Speaking Fundamentals benefits different students in different ways. The instructor needs to know a bit more about you in order to tailor aspects of the course to your unique interests and needs.

Your Name: _____ Section: _____

Telephone Number: _____ Email: _____

1. What are two goals you can identify that you hope to gain from taking this class?

2. What is/are your academic areas of interest?

3. Describe your writing ability.

4. Describe your speaking ability.

5. What experience(s) have you had with public speaking?

6. Do you enjoy/fear/avoid speaking in front of groups? Why or why not?

7. What special interests or hobbies do you have?

8. What sorts of things do you enjoy reading?

9. What are your favorite television programs? Why?

10. In what occupation are you most interested?

11. What do you plan to be doing five years from now?

12. What are your pet peeves?

13. Do you have any special needs I should know about?

PUBLIC SPEAKING BASICS

ANXIETY AND PUBLIC SPEAKING

PRPSA (PERSONAL REPORT OF PUBLIC SPEAKING ANXIETY)

Goal: This exercise will reveal your level of anxiety on a scale ranging from low, to moderately low, to moderate, to moderately high, to high.

Rationale: Since about 3/4 of the United States population experiences anxiety, you probably already know whether you feel anxious about speaking in public. What you may not realize, however, is how many of your classmates feel the same way. This activity provides a means by which to illustrate the pervasive nature of public speaking anxiety. In other words, you are NOT alone.

Directions: The following is composed of thirty-four statements concerning feelings about communicating with other people. Indicate the degree to which the statements apply to you by marking whether you (1) strongly agree, (2) agree, (3) are undecided, (4) disagree, or (5) strongly disagree with each statement. Work quickly; just record your first impression.

_____ 1. While preparing a speech I feel tense and nervous.

_____ 2. 1 feel tense when I see the words *speech* and *public speech* on a course outline when studying.

_____ 3. My thoughts become confused and jumbled when I am giving a speech.

_____ 4. Right after giving a speech I feel that I have had a pleasant experience.

_____ 5. 1 get anxious when I think about an upcoming speech.

_____ 6. 1 have no fear of giving a speech.

_____ 7. Although I am nervous just before starting a speech, I soon settle down after starting and feel calm and comfortable.

_____ 8. I look forward to giving a speech.

_____ 9. When the instructor announces a speaking assignment in class I can feel myself getting tense.

_____ 10. My hands tremble when I am giving a speech.

_____ 11. I feel relaxed while giving a speech.

_____ 12. I enjoy preparing for a speech.

_____ 13. I am in constant fear of forgetting what I prepared to say.

_____ 14. I get anxious if someone asks me something about my topic that I do not know.

_____ 15. I face the prospect of giving a speech with confidence.

_____ 16. I feel that I am in complete possession of myself while giving a speech.

_____ 17. My mind is clear when giving a speech.

_____ 18. I do not dread giving a speech.

_____ 19. I perspire just before starting a speech.

_____ 20. My heart beats very fast just as I start a speech.

_____ 21. I experience considerable anxiety while sitting in the room just before my speech starts.

_____ 22. Certain parts of my body feel very tense and rigid while giving a speech.

_____ 23. Realizing that only a little time remains in a speech makes me very tense and anxious.

_____ 24. While giving a speech I know I can control my feelings of tension and stress.

_____ 25. I breathe faster just before starting a speech.

_____ 26. I feet comfortable and relaxed in the hour or so just before giving a speech.

_____ 27. I do poorer on speeches because I am anxious.

_____ 28. I feel anxious when the teacher announces the date of a speaking assignment.

_____ 29. When I make a mistake while giving a speech, I find it hard to concentrate on the parts that follow.

_____ 30. During an important speech I experience a feeling of helplessness building up inside me.

_____ 31. I have trouble falling asleep the night before a speech.

_____ 32. My heart beats very fast while I present a speech.

____ 33. I feel anxious while waiting to give my speech.

____ 34. While giving a speech I get so nervous I forget facts I really know.

To determine your score on the PRPSA[1], complete the following steps:

1. Add the scores for items 1, 2, 3, 5, 9, 10, 13, 14, 19, 20, 21, 22, 23, 25, 27, 28, 29, 30, 31, 32, 33, and 34.

2. Add the scores for items 4, 6, 7, 8, 11, 12, 15, 16, 17, 18, 24, and 26.

3. Complete the following formula: PRPSA = 132 − (total from step 1) + (total from step 2).

4. Your score on the PRPSA can range between 34 and 170:

   34–84 indicate a very low anxiety about public speaking.
   85–92 indicate a moderately low level of anxiety about public speaking.
   93–110 suggests moderate anxiety in most public speaking situations but not so severe that the individual cannot cope and be a successful speaker.
   111–119 suggest a moderately high anxiety about public speaking. People with such scores will tend to avoid public speaking.
   120–170 indicate a very high anxiety about public speaking. People with these scores will go to considerable lengths to avoid all types of public speaking situations.

Computing Your Score:

A: _____(TOTAL FROM ADDING #1 RESULTS)

B: _____(TOTAL FROM ADDING #2 RESULTS)

   (132   −   A)   +   B   =   _____
                                    (PRPSA)

[1]The PRPSA was taken from McCroskey and Virginia P. Richmond, *Communication: Apprehension, Avoidance, and Effectiveness*, Fourth Edition (Scottsdale, AZ: Gorsuch Scarisbrick, Publishers, 1995) pp. 131–132. Reprinted with permission of the publisher.

26

COPING WITH ANXIETY

What Can You Do to Control Your Speech Anxiety?

1. **Be prepared to speak.** One of the biggest causes of speech anxiety is lack of preparation. If you think you can research a topic, organize your materials, type your outline, prepare your notes, practice your speech without relying on your notes, and incorporate a visual aid or object, *on the night before you are scheduled to speak*, you most certainly *will* have speech anxiety.

2. **Focus on your message.** If you concentrate on getting your message across to the listener rather than thinking about what your audience is thinking of you, you should experience less speech anxiety.

3. **Nobody "bats" 1000!** Understanding that you will make some mistakes while speaking should help you to keep the speaking situation in perspective. The important thing about the speech experience is that the audience *wants* you to succeed. As a speaker, let the little mistakes go by—there is very little you can do once they occur—and keep the main ideas coming through clearly. When your speech is over, your audience will most likely not even remember what you thought were "major league" errors.

4. **Never apologize for your nervousness.** Although some beginning speakers believe alerting an audience to their nervousness will enhance their effectiveness, it is not true. Letting listeners know about our nervousness usually causes them to focus on our symptoms of nervousness rather than on our message.

5. **Keep the speech in perspective.** After all, the speech is simply "a speech." When it is over you should still be breathing. Your life will go on as it did before you spoke. Try not to put additional pressure on yourself by overemphasizing the importance of the speaking opportunity.

6. **Try mental and physical exercises to help reduce your speech anxiety.** There are many exercises you might try to reduce your speech anxiety that include mental and physical exercises. Try thinking of your favorite spot—a quiet place where you have peace and solitude for a few minutes just before you get up to speak. Although certain strenuous physical exercises help relieve the stress of having to speak, they are not always possible moments before you must speak in a class or public meeting. As such, try isometric exercises which might involve making a tight grip with your hands, pressing your fingers or palms together, or pushing your heels together prior to speaking. Taking a deep breath before rising to speak also releases pent up nervousness.

7. **Monitor your speech anxiety while you speak.** Even though you might feel as if the entire class were observing your knees shaking or hearing your voice quiver, usually the speech anxiety you experience is not as obvious as you might think. You might try to gesture or even move from one point to another in front of your audience. Pushing down on your big toes—without locking your knees—while speaking can also help to drive your nervousness right out.

8. **As a safeguard, build a visual aid and/or physical activity into your speech.** Showing the object or visual aid will help you concentrate more on your speech and less on your nervousness.

LEARNING STYLES AND PUBLIC SPEAKING

The concept of learning styles differences has been receiving a great deal of attention by educational psychologists during recent years. Communication researchers have only begun to realize that how you address learning styles in your public speeches makes a difference in terms of how effectively you reach your listeners. For listeners to grasp the content of your speeches most effectively, it is necessary to present information visually, orally, and actively. It is also necessary to present ideas in ways that address each of four different stages of learning. Doing so ensures that you are reaching the diverse preferences represented in your audience.

FOUR STAGES OF LEARNING

There are a number of theories about learning styles. Kolb's (1984) theory is probably the most widely accepted model available at this time. He claims that when we learn, we actually go through a series of four stages. In order to process our experiences, we must experience each of these four stages of understanding. Different people, however, prefer to spend more time in one particular stage rather than the others.

Stage 1:

During Stage 1, we are looking for reasons for learning information. We try to discover personal connections with the content.

Typical Questions: Why are we learning this? How will learning this help us in other aspects of our lives? Where does this occur?

In Terms of Public Speaking: Listeners engaged in Stage 1 are looking for *listener relevance links, as well as examples where these ideas occur in a variety of real life contexts.*

Stage 2:

During Stage 2, we are striving to absorb the information presented. We have already decided we want to learn the information. In this stage, we are eager to learn simply for the sheer pleasure of learning.

Typical Questions: What strategies, ideas, techniques, or methods are important? What are the important facts? What is important to remember?

In Terms of Public Speaking: Listeners engaged in Stage 2 are looking for lots of facts, definitions, and explanations (cited effectively). They are looking for information that is presented in an orderly and concise manner.

Stage 3:

During Stage 3, we are desiring opportunities to experiment with the ideas presented. We want to see if these "facts" really work in daily life. We want to know about specific examples and applications of these ideas in the real world.

Typical Questions: Is this idea usable? Can I *use* this information to improve my own current situation? What are some practical applications of these ideas?

In Terms of Public Speaking: Listeners engaged in Stage 3 are looking for specific applications of the idea. They are looking for the bottom line. What's a workable solution to a problem? What is the best answer?

Stage 4:

During Stage 4, we are concerned about how we can use what we learn to make our lives better and the world a better place. We want to engage with others in group activities, conversations, and interactions.

Typical Questions: Where *else* in my life could I use this information or skill? How do these ideas help me understand other aspects of my life and of the world as a whole? What do other people think about these ideas?

In Terms of Public Speaking: Listeners engaged in Stage 4 are looking for places where the concept can be extended beyond knowledge and understanding and beyond application to extensions and integrations with other fields of study, with other areas of life, and with other people's lives. They are looking for well-developed conclusions that may even raise additional questions.

FOUR PREFERRED LEARNING STYLES

Diverger: If you prefer to learn in the ways described in Stage 1, you are a diverger. Although you also learn in other ways, this is your preferred learning style. You prefer learning things that you feel are important and relevant to you today. You look for personal meaning. You like to consider a variety of perspectives on a topic. You enjoy "feeling" and "watching."

Assimilator: If you prefer to learn in the ways described in Stage 2, you are an assimilator. Although you also learn in other ways, this is your preferred learning style. You like to take the time to plan things out and understand the details of material accurately. You look for orderly and detailed presentation of information. You enjoy "watching" and "thinking."

Converger: If you prefer to learn in the ways described in Stage 3, you are a converger. Although you also learn in other ways, this is your preferred learning style. You like to see direct application of ideas to real life situations. You like to get to the "bottom line." You enjoy "thinking" and "doing."

Accommodator: If you prefer to learn in the ways described in Stage 4, you are an accommodator. Although you also learn in other ways, this is your preferred learning style. You like to practice what you have learned. You like hands-on activities. You like connecting with others to consider ways of extending ideas. You like to come up with new questions. You enjoy "doing" and "feeling."

Remember that each listener may *prefer* learning in a particular way; however, all listeners benefit from messages that address each learning style stage and round the entire cycle of learning.

THE LEARNING CYCLE

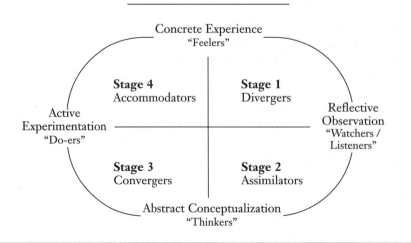

KOLB'S PREFERRED LEARNING STYLE
PERSONAL INVENTORY

Goal: This exercise will reveal the style of learning you prefer. We all tend to learn in four general ways, however, each of us tends to prefer a certain style.

Rationale: It is important to develop the ability to learn material in a variety of ways. Different members of your audience will better grasp your ideas when presented in a manner that addresses their preferred learning style. Beginning public speakers, however, tend to present ideas in ways that address their own preferred learning style. This comes at the expense of reaching those listeners who learn better when material is presented in a different way. By first understanding your own preferred learning style, you can better develop speeches that present material in a variety of ways in order to address the diverse learning styles represented in your listeners and to round the entire cycle of learning.

Learning Styles Quiz

STEP 1: For each question, circle the letter next to the response that is most like you. Remember there are *no wrong answers*. Work quickly. Record your first thought.

(1) When I purchase a kit where some assembly is required, I am most likely to begin by:
    a. soliciting advice and possibly help from someone who has put together a similar item in the past.
    b. studying the pieces, diagram, and picture of the item on the package or box.
    c. reading through all of the directions.
    d. putting the item together, referring to the directions only when I get stuck.

(2) I am most likely to try making a new recipe when:
    a. I can taste it myself first.
    b. I see a picture of it in a magazine or on television.
    c. I read through a recipe for it.
    d. I want to try changing it in some way.

(3) When I make decisions, I usually rely most on my:
    a. feelings.
    b. observations.
    c. thoughts.
    d. actions.

(4) I tend to enjoy classes most where:
    a. students interact with each other often.
    b. professors use a lot of visual aids.
    c. professors lecture most of the time.
    d. students apply concepts directly with activities.

(5) I tend to be persuaded most when:
    a. I am presented with actual examples and experiences of people.
    b. I have time to reflect about what I hear.
    c. I am presented with specific facts and statistics related to the issue.
    d. I experience issues first-hand.

(6) If I were asked to choose only one, I'd say I am:
    a. intuitive.
    b. careful.
    c. logical.
    d. responsible.

(7) I am most likely to enjoy participating in extra-curricular activities and functions:
   a. that are new and different.
   b. that allow me to observe for awhile before joining in.
   c. that require logical analysis.
   d. that let me be actively involved.

(8) I prefer working in an environment where:
   a. I can interact with others.
   b. I am able to take time to reflect.
   c. I am challenged to analyze logically.
   d. I have opportunities to apply concepts and try things out.

(9) I especially dislike classes where the main thing is:
   a. professors lecturing about abstract concepts.
   b. students doing lots of activities.
   c. students engaging in open-ended discussions.
   d. students taking lots of notes.

(10) When discussing ideas with others, I am best at:
   a. considering a variety of points of view.
   b. taking time to reflect before responding.
   c. using logic to analyze and evaluate.
   d. getting things done and accomplishing goals.

(11) When learning a new computer software program, I am most likely to begin by:
   a. asking for advice from people who've used the program before
   b. following the directions carefully.
   c. reading through the manual.
   d. experimenting with the program and using the manual only when I get stuck.

(12) When I take a vacation, I particularly enjoy:
   a. getting to know the people who live there and learn from them about their customs and experiences.
   b. taking time to plan each day carefully.
   c. reading as much as possible about each place while I'm there.
   d. experimenting with and trying out new customs, foods, and experiences.

STEP 2: Count up the number of "a," "b," "c," and "d" responses you circled and record them in the space provided:

   A =_____   B =_____   C = _____   D =_____

If you circled mostly As, you tend to prefer to learn by **feeling.**
If you circled mostly Bs, you tend to prefer to learn by **watching.**
If you circled mostly Cs, you tend to prefer to learn by **thinking.**
If you circled mostly Ds, you tend to prefer to learn by **doing.**

STEP 3: Add together the scores you got in STEP 2 as follows:

   A + B = _____
   B + C = _____
   C + D =_____
   A + D = _____

STEP 4: Circle the highest of the four sums you got in STEP 3.

If you circled the A + B score:
You tend to be a **diverger.** You prefer to learn by some combination of watching and feeling.

If you circled the B + C score:
You tend to be an **assimilator.** You prefer to learn by some combination of watching and thinking.

If you circled the C + D score:
You tend to be a **converger.** You prefer to learn by some combination of thinking and doing.

If you circled the A + D score:
You tend to be an **accommodator.** You prefer to learn by some combination of doing and feeling.

STEP 5: Consider how you will approach the speech preparation and presentation process in ways that address all of these learning styles. Remember, each learning style represents one stage on the cycle.

Diverger (Stage 1 preference): You probably want to know why you are learning things. You seek a personal connection with the content. So, one of your public speaking strengths is the ability to articulate *listener relevance links*. You also like to consider things from many points of view. Another public speaking strength is your use of *examples*, *testimonies*, and *quotations* from *interviews* with real people in your speeches. (If you're a converger, you'll need to be sure to include these things in your speeches as well.)

Assimilator (Stage 2 preference): You are likely to enjoy absorbing lots of information and strive for an understanding of *what* it means. Your public speaking strengths lie in providing clear *facts, statistics, definitions,* and *explanations,* and in arranging them in a logical and orderly fashion. (If you're an accommodator, you'll need to be sure to include these things in your speeches as well.)

Converger (Stage 3 preference): You probably like to see if the facts you learn actually work in daily life. You want to know how an idea, strategy, or method works by trying it out. Your public speaking strengths lie in providing *practical applications* for using information to improve current situations, as well as in conceptualizing a *workable solution* to a problem. (If you're a diverger, you'll need to be sure to include these things in your speeches as well.)

Accommodator (Stage 4 preference): You like to take what you've discovered and figure out *where else* you can use it to *make a difference* in your life and the lives of others. You public speaking strengths lie in your ability to come up with *new solutions* to old problems. You enjoy interacting with others and probably excel at *delivering* your speech dynamically. (If you're an assimilator, you'll need to be sure to include these things in your speech as well.)

ADDRESSING DIVERSE LEARNING STYLES

To be most effective as a public speaker, you must present your ideas in a variety of ways that address the different learning styles represented in your audience. You can safely assume that not all listeners prefer the same learning style as you do. You also realize that the most effective learning is the kind that takes listeners through each of the four stages of the learning cycle. So, avoid the temptation to rely too heavily on presenting material geared mainly toward your own preferred learning style. Doing so both ignores the needs of those listeners who do not share your preferred learning style and fails to present ideas that take listeners through the four-stage cycle of learning.

There are specific strategies you ought to employ when researching, when preparing and outlining, and when rehearsing your speech to help insure that your public speech addresses a variety of learning styles.

1. **When researching:** Collect supporting material that comes from a variety of different resources. Use library materials, personal interviews, and surveys. Also, collect a variety of kinds of supporting material, such as examples and stories, definitions and explanations, personal testimonies, facts and statistics, and analogies that compare or contrast your ideas with related information.

2. **When preparing and outlining:** Consider the needs of some learners to follow an orderly pattern of thought. Consider presenting your ideas with the help of visual, audio, and audiovisual aids. Visual aids may help "watchers" grasp ideas. Aids that show real life contexts may help "feelers." Aids that present multiple perspectives may help "thinkers." Aids that encourage interaction may help "doers." Consider using listener relevance links throughout the speech to clarify how your topic may be applied in listeners' real life experiences. Consider incorporating an experiential opportunity for listeners to try during or after the presentation.

3. **When rehearsing:** Practice using emotional conviction in your voice to address "feelers." Practice using gestures and facial expressions to address "feelers" and "watchers." Practice using your visual aids effectively for "watchers" and "thinkers." Practice talking through an activity or experiential activity to address the "doers."

In sum, diversity and variety in supporting material, structural methods, and presentational style all contribute to moving listeners effectively through the four stages of learning. Doing so also ensures a public speech that addresses the different preferred learning styles of your listeners.

MAJOR COMPONENTS OF PUBLIC SPEAKING

Effective public speaking is centered on three major areas: delivery, structure, and content. If you can master skills in each of these areas, you can become a competent communicator in public speaking situations.

DELIVERY

Effective delivery means you employ effective use of voice *and* effective use of body.

Use of Voice

1. First, effective use of voice means being intelligible. In other words, do you use an appropriate rate, volume, and pitch those helps listeners understand what you are saying?

2. In addition to intelligibility, you need to sound conversational. To clarify, do you sound like you are talking with your listeners rather than presenting in front of them or reading to them?

3. You also need to sound fluent. You need crisp articulation, enunciation, and pronunciation. Your phrases should sound smoothly connected rather than choppy and disconnected.

4. Effective use of voice also means using vocal variety in ways that make you sound committed to the topic and occasion. If your speech is something you are excited about, you ought to sound excited. If it is a serious speech, you ought to sound serious. If it is humorous, you ought to sound like you are having fun with it. You achieve this by incorporating vocal variety–changes in pitch, rate, volume, and use of stresses and pauses.

Use of Body

1. Effective use of body means being poised. Do you appear confident, comfortable and "in control?"

2. Effective use of body also has to do with attire. You should dress up a bit more than your listeners dress in order to appear credible and committed.

3. You also need to avoid engaging in distracting nonverbal cues such as fidgeting with your notes, playing with your hair, or shifting and swaying. These actions need to be avoided because they can distract listeners from the message and "leak" nervousness.

4. Effective use of body also means using effective eye contact. Doing so means using direct eye contact, looking listeners in the eye as opposed to over their heads. It also means spanning the entire room (even the corners and edges), turning your entire head as you do so. Finally, it means relying on your notes less than 10 percent of the time. These notes are a speaking outline comprised of key words, phrases, and delivery cues. Your reliance on them should be minimal.

5. Effective use of body also means using facial expressions, gestures, and motivated movement only in ways that *reinforce* the verbal message. They should reinforce an emotional attitude or clarify structure. If they do not, they are distracting nonverbal cues and should be eliminated.

CONTENT

To have good content, you need to consider the purpose of your speech and make sure your message adheres to that purpose. In other words, if you are presenting an informative speech, be sure you are not trying to get listeners to change their behavior. Likewise, if your purpose is an actuation persuasive speech, be sure to provide an action step telling listeners what they should do to eliminate the problem or improve the situation. Your analysis should also offer reasoning that is rooted in ethos (ethical appeals), pathos (emotional appeals), and logos (logical appeals). You can also achieve this by making sure your speech rounds the entire cycle of learning, that is, addresses feeling, thinking, watching, and doing.

Make sure your supporting material is varied, accurate, evenly distributed, and properly credited. Finally, offer breadth, depth, and listener relevance links throughout the speech; that is, consider these elements *for each main point*. Listener relevance links are statements that remind listeners how your information relates to some aspect of their life. As a goal, answer this question for each main point: How will listeners benefit from hearing this?

STRUCTURE

Effective structure means offering your ideas in an orderly framework so listeners can follow your train of thought. Macrostructural elements have to do with the elements of the outline itself. Microstructural elements have to do with language choices you make to articulate your ideas. Language should be accurate, clear, inclusive, and vivid. You should avoid language that marginalizes or stereotypes members of your audience. You should also only use technical jargon when you define it in simple language. And you should avoid using slang terms or "verbal garbage" (uhms, uhs, like, and ya know) to fill pauses in the presentation. The following is a "Generic Public Speech Outline," which explains the macrostructural components of an effective public speech.

GENERIC PUBLIC SPEECH STRUCTURE

Regardless of the general purpose of your speech, there are several elements which remain consistent. In order for listeners to follow your train of thinking, always try to adhere to the "golden rule" of public speaking. (*i.e.*, 1. Tell them what you're going to tell them. 2. Tell them. 3. Tell them what you told them.) These macrostructural elements are described in the following sample outline form.

SAMPLE OUTLINE

Introduction

The introduction should serve to set up the rest of the speech for listeners. (In the "golden rule" of public speaking this is the "Tell them what you're going to tell them" part.)

I. **Attention Catcher** (This statement serves two functions: it catches listeners' attention and tunes them into your topic. You may use a rhetorical question, a direct question, a humorous anecdote, a famous quotation, a hypothetical example, an actual example, a startling statistic, and so on.)

II. **Listener Relevance** (Once you have your listeners' attention, you need to reveal why they should listen to this particular speech. How does this material affect them? Why should they care?)

III. **Speaker Credibility** (In this step, you need to let listeners know why they should listen to you in particular. How/Why do you know more about this topic than they do? You may have personal experience with the topic; you may have researched extensively; you may have written articles about the topic. The point is, let your listeners know at the outset that you know a good deal about the topic.)

IV. **Thesis Statement** (This one-sentence summary of your speech is formed by, first, combining the general purpose to inform, to persuade, to entertain, to introduce, and the specific purpose about what? Be sure to state your thesis quite clearly. If listeners miss this part, they will have difficulty following the rest of the speech.)

V. **Preview** (In this statement, alert your listeners to the main points of your speech. As with the thesis statement, be very clear so listeners can easily follow the organizational pattern of the speech.)

Body

(In the "golden rule," this is the "Tell them." part.)

I. **First main point**

A. Subpoint (These supporting points help listeners understand your perspective. They learn why you stated your main point in the way you did. Consider breadth, depth, and listener relevance as you support each main point.)

B. Subpoint

Transition (Verbally tie the two main points together, in this case the first and second main points, so that listeners know you're moving forward structurally.)

II. **Second main point**

    A. Subpoint

    B. Subpoint

Transition (Verbally tie the second and third main points together to create a sense of forward motion.)

III. **Third main point**

    A. Subpoint

    B. Subpoint

Conclusion

(This serves the "golden rule" function of telling them "what you told them."

I. **Thesis Restatement** (You may simply use the Thesis statement from the introduction, changing it to past tense.)

II. **Summarize Main Point** (Remind listeners of the two to four main points about which you elaborated during the speech.)

III. **Clincher** (The clincher serves several functions: provides closure, often ties back to the attention catcher, heightens speech to aid in retention, helps listeners remember. . . . "Thank you" is NOT a clincher.)

References

Cite sources just as you would for a written paper, using complete references. Refer to the APA style guide for appropriate format.

ETHICAL CONCERNS IN PUBLIC SPEAKING

CONSIDERING SOURCES

Most of you are not "experts" on your speech topics. As a result, you need to enhance your credibility by including supporting material from experts in the body of your speech. In order to truly enhance your credibility and to avoid plagiarism, you need to document the sources of your information in the reference list at the end of your formal outline and during the speech itself.

REFERENCE LIST CITATIONS

You will be expected to acknowledge sources as you sue them in your speech. In addition, you must attach a list of your sources to the outline you submit to your instructor. The form for listing sources in your *Reference List* should follow the suggested guidelines of a style manual. We require source citations that adhere to the guidelines of the *Publication Manual of the American Psychological Association* (5th ed.). Refer to Chapter 7 in your textbook as you prepare your reference list.

ORAL FOOTNOTE CITATIONS

It is important to acknowledge when you are drawing upon the words and thoughts of others during the oral presentation, as well. Usually, such source citations occur immediately before you actually quote the source. After the quotation has been shared, you usually signal the listener that you are no longer quoting from the source. A short pause immediately before and immediately after the quotation can serve as nonverbal quotation marks for the listener. While there is nothing wrong with using "quote" and "unquote" as a means of acknowledging the presence of material attributed to another, doing so lacks artistry.

Acknowledgment of the source can be accomplished in a variety of ways. As a general rule, try to cite enough information about the source so that listeners may locate the source themselves. "Oral footnotes" cited aloud during the oral performance might be worded in any of the following ways:

Internet document

Be sure to indicate the author or organization posting the document (as well as their credentials). Also indicate the date of the posting. It is not necessary to include the path in your oral footnote.

> "North Dakota State University, a leading agricultural research institution, published a document on the internet on December 21, 1997. According to that document. . . ."

> "Sprung writes online in the May 11, 1998, *In-Forum* that. . . "

> "Nakata and Sivakumar, in their January 1996 article found online in the *Journal of Marketing*, maintain . . ."

Interview

> "Wahlberg, director of public affairs at North Dakota State University, indicated during a personal interview on April 28, 1998, that . . ."

Journal or Magazine Article

"According to a May/June 1998 article in *Health* magazine . . . ."

Book

"In her 2000 edition of *The Process of Public Speaking*, Sellnow wrote . . ."

You may use additional formats in oral footnotes as long as you adhere to the rule of providing listeners enough information to look the material up themselves if they choose to do so. Refer to Chapter 7 in your textbook for additional examples.

Name: _____ Section: _____

USING THE LIBRARY

Goal: This assignment is designed to help you learn where different library resources are located in the library, how to write the source citation using APA style, and how to cite the source as an oral footnote in a speech.

Rationale: Students are often unfamiliar with the various locations of sources in the library. They are also uncertain about the format for citing those source in the reference list and during the speech itself. This assignment provides students an opportunity to practice citing sources before doing an actual graded speech.

Directions: For each of the following topics, write the full source citation in APA style and provide an oral footnote example in the space provided.

Examples:

(A) Written Citation:

Langewiesche, W. (1998). The lessons of ValuJet 592. *The Atlantic Monthly, 281,* 81–98.

(B) Oral Footnote:

"According to Langewiesche, in a 1998 issue of *The Atlantic Monthly,....*"

TOPIC #1: TOBACCO LEGISLATION

BOOK

(A)

(B)

PERIODICAL

(A)

(B)

40

INTERNET SOURCE

(A)

(B)

NEWSPAPER

(A)

(B)

TOPIC #2: GUN CONTROL

BOOK

(A)

(B)

PERIODICAL

(A)

(B)

INTERNET SOURCE

(A)

(B)

CONSIDERING BIAS

As a speaker, your choice of language is a powerful tool which can have both positive and negative effects upon your credibility. The use of biased language may alienate listeners, reducing your effectiveness as a speaker. The following suggestions are taken from the 4th edition of the *Publication Manual of the American Psychological Association* (Washington, D.C.: APA, 1994), pp. 46–60.

Guideline 1: Be specific to avoid stereotypic bias.

Problematic:	**Preferred:**
The client's behavior was typically female	The client's behavior was [specify].

Guideline 2: Be sensitive to labels.

Problematic:	**Preferred:**
There were 300 Orientals.	There were 300 Asian participants.
The elderly	Older people
Girls and men	Women and men

Guideline 3: Acknowledge participation.

Problematic:	**Preferred:**
Our study included 60 subjects.	Sixty people participated in our study.
The client is usually the best judge of his experience.	The client is usually the best judge of his or her experience.
Man, mankind	People, humanity, human beings
Manpower	Workforce, personnel, workers
Researchers often neglect their wives and children	Researchers often neglect their spouses and children
Woman doctor, lady lawyer, male nurse, woman driver	Doctor, lawyer, nurse, driver
Mothering	Parenting, nurturing
Chairman	Chair, Chairperson
Foreman, mailman, fireman	Supervisor, postal worker, firefighter
Mrs. John Smith	Jane Smith
Women reported lesbian sexual fantasies	Women reported female-female sexual fantasies
Disabled person	Person with a disability
Mentally ill person	Person with a mental illness
Epileptics	Individuals with epilepsy
The learnings disabled	Children with a learning disability
Strike victim	Person who had a stroke
Confined to a wheelchair	Uses a wheelchair

INCLUSIVE LANGUAGE

For those students who have never been asked to use inclusive language in oral and written communication, the task might seem formidable at first. Inclusiveness means sharing, not limiting experience. This means we must learn to both value and benefit from the gifts, talents, and insights of all human beings including women, men, Blacks, Hispanics, Asians, Europeans, Native Americans, young, old, physically disadvantaged, and so on. The following guidelines are offered as the groundwork for becoming an inclusive speaker.

1. Recast the statement in the plural:

   From: Each student must complete his formal outline.

   To: Students must complete their formal outlines.

2. Replace third-person singular possessives with articles which include both genders:

   From: Each student completed his formal outline.

   To: Each student completed a formal outline.

3. Avoid using categorical judgments which demean individuals as though that term described the person's complete identity. (*i.e.*, blind, crippled, etc.)

4. Be aware of the names which members of various ethnic, political, and religious groups prefer for themselves. (*i.e.*, Native American/Indian, Black/Negro, feminist/ women's libber, etc.)

CULTURAL DIVERSITY

As the global community shrinks, the issue of diversity is becoming increasingly significant in American society. The government, the media, organizations, and individuals are exploring the impact of this diversity. Specifically, if we are to effectively address contemporary societal issues and needs, we must "hear" the voices of all those who comprise that society. There exist a variety·of interpretations for "cultural diversity." The definition adhered to in this book maintains that differences based on age, education, gender, spiritual practice, race, family status, ethnicity, social and economic class, sexual orientation, geographic location, military experience and physical and mental health/ability are all elements of cultural diversity (p. 3). Loden and Rosener (1991) write that:

> humans come in a variety of sizes, shapes and colors. This variety helps to differentiate us from each other. While we share the important dimension of humanness with all members of our species, there are biological and environmental differences that separate and distinguish us as individuals and groups. From an objective point of view, it is this vast array of physical and cultural differences that constitute the spectrum of human diversity. From the subjective point of view, diversity is otherness or those human qualities that are different from our own and outside the groups to which we belong, yet present in other individuals and groups. Others, then, are people who are different from us along one of several dimensions. (p. 18)

Primary dimensions are those immutable human differences that form the core of our individual identities including age, ethnicity, gender, physical abilities/qualities, race and sexual/affectional orientation. Secondary dimensions can be—and often are—changed throughout our lives; including background, geographic location, income, marital status, military experience, parental status, religious beliefs, work experience, and so on. These primary and secondary dimensions work together to shape each individual's experiences, values, and perceptions.

In terms of public speaking, we must be considerate and inclusive of all individuals and their experiences, values, and perceptions. We can do this by acknowledging our values, beliefs, and biases as our own; and not assume they are shared by others. We can also do this by using a public speaking assignment as an opportunity to reveal an aspect or issue which characterizes us (or someone else) as a part of a culturally diverse group.

Cultural diversity is broadly defined as those differences arising out of issues of ability/disability, age, ethnicity, gender, race, regional difference, sexual orientation, or worldview. Cultural diversity can be globally conceived as when related to nationality, race, and ethnicity. It can also be perceived within the United States such as African Americans, Native Americans, individuals who are disabled, individuals who are gay, older Americans, and so forth.

Cultural diversity is most often conceived in comparison to or as it contrasts with the dominant culture. Dominant culture is defined as the attitudes, values, and beliefs held by the group in power. The dominant culture in the United States, for example, is Euroamerican, middle-class males.

CRITIQUING PUBLIC SPEECHES

When you critique a public speaker, you are actually going beyond merely evaluating the worth of their message, organization, and performance. As a critic, you also offer the speaker suggestions for improving their message, organization, and performance. You can do this by indicating specific aspects that the speaker did well (in your opinion), as well as discussing specific aspects that the speaker should do differently (in your opinion).

ETHICAL CONSIDERATIONS

To be an ethical critic, there are certain things you "ought to" do in your critique. Whereas a critique basically only needs to offer suggestions for improvement, an ethical critique both highlights specific strengths of the speaker's message, organization, and delivery and offers suggestions for improvement. Moreover, an ethical critique explains why you view the aspect as a strength or a weakness and suggests methods indicating how a speaker could make the suggested change. Suggestions are also offered in a tone of respect, usually using "I" language. An ethical critique offers strengths and suggestions about the speaker's delivery, structure, and content. What follows are examples of unethical and ethical critiques in each of these areas.

UNETHICAL DELIVERY CRITIQUES

1. "Good eye contact."

This is unethical because it is so vague that the speaker does not really know what to improve. He or she does not know what it is about her or his eye contact that is "good" or why eye contact is a strength.

2. "Slow down."

This is unethical because it is so vague that the speaker does not know why to change or why the rate was problematic. The speaker also is not offered any methods to try for slowing down the rate. And the critique is unethical because the advice is not phrased in a tone of respect, using "I" language.

ETHICAL DELIVERY CRITIQUES

1. "Good eye contact. You looked me in the eye so I felt like you were really talking to me. It made me feel included in the communication interaction. I wanted to listen to you."

2. "At times you spoke so quickly that I missed your information. For example, I did not catch the percentages of teenage dropouts you talked about. If you slowed down, it would be easier for me to catch information. Maybe you could practice into a tape recorder to hear where you speed up too much."

UNETHICAL STRUCTURE CRITIQUES

1. "Good attention catcher."

This is unethical because it is so vague that the speaker does not really know what to improve. He or she does not know what it is about her or his attention catcher that is "good" or why her or his attention catcher is a strength.

2. "Didn't hear transitions."

This is unethical because it is so vague that the speaker does not know why to change transitions or why the transitions were unclear. The speaker also is not offered any methods for improvement. And the critique is unethical because the advice is not phrased in a tone of respect, using "I" language.

ETHICAL STRUCTURE CRITIQUES

1. "Your attention catcher was good. The humorous story made me laugh and caught my attention. It was also about daycare which set up the topic of your speech well. Good job!"

2. "I didn't catch the transition between the second and third main point. Maybe I just missed it. Perhaps you could try verbally tieing the two points together more bluntly and pause before and after the transition statement. Then, people like me would be less likely to miss it."

UNETHICAL CONTENT CRITIQUES

1. "Interesting points."

This is unethical because it is so vague that the speaker does not really know what to improve. He or she does not know what it is about her or his points that are "good" or why the points are a strength.

2. "Too many statistics."

This is unethical because it is so vague that the speaker does not know why to change or why the statistics were problematic. The speaker is also not offered any methods for improving the use of statistics. And the critique is unethical because the advice is not phrased in a tone of respect, using "I" language.

ETHICAL CONTENT CRITIQUES

1. "Your second main point was really interesting. I hadn't thought about how influential television commercials can be on our perceptions of what is "normal" and "abnormal.""

2. "I had a hard time remembering all the statistics you provided. I'm sure they are interesting, but there were so many and they were so specific that I got lost. Maybe you could also show them on a visual aid. Maybe you could also round them off. Instead of saying '37.6%,' you could say 'about 40%' or 'almost half.' This way, I could grasp your main ideas better."

FORENSICS SPEECH CRITIQUE FORM

Name _____Section _____Date _____

Tournament or Event Attended _____

Speaker _____

Topic _____

     Either—Event Attendance: _____Program Attached _____

     Or—Tournament Attendance: _____

     This certifies that the above student was
     present for this round of speeches.

     Judge's Signature _____

     Judge's School _____

Discuss the following questions and cite specific examples to support your conclusion:

1. What was the speaker's purpose?

2. How did the speaker relate his/her topic to the audience?

3. What type of supporting materials did the speaker use to develop the topic?

4. Were the supporting materials interesting and convincing?

5. In what way was the speaker's delivery effective?

6. In what way was the speaker's delivery ineffective?

7. If you were the speaker, what would you have done differently and why?

PROFESSIONAL SPEAKER CRITIQUE

Goal: This assignment provides you an opportunity to critique the delivery skills, structure, and content of a professional speaker.

Rationale: Students need opportunities to apply what they are learning in the classroom to real life situations (Stage 3). This can make material and skills more meaningful. Just as some student speakers are more skilled than others, so are some professional speakers more skilled than others. This assignment provides students an opportunity to discover for themselves how professional speakers do an do not adhere to the "rules" of effective public speaking.

Directions: Complete a 1–2 page typed, double-spaced critique of a professional public speaker. Address aspects of audience analysis (see page 51), nature and purpose of the occasion, delivery (strengths and weaknesses), structure (strengths and weaknesses), and content (strengths and weaknesses) in your paper. Be sure to include accurate public speaking terminology in your critique where appropriate.

You will be required to turn in a completed audience assessment form (p. 51) and proof of attendance (i.e., program or brochure) with your critique.

Questions you might consider as you listen. These may serve as supporting material for your critique as you prepare it.

1. Who was the speaker? What are his or her credentials?

2. Where did he or she speak? Was the room "good" or "bad" and why?

3. Did the speaker show signs of public speaking anxiety?

4. Did the speaker use notes? Did he or she sound conversational? How did that influence his or her effectiveness?

5. Consider delivery (use of voice and body). What did the speaker do well and why?

6. Consider delivery (use of voice and body). What could the speaker do better and why?

7. Consider structure. What did the speaker do well and why?

8. Consider structure. What could the speaker do better and why?

9. Consider content. What did the speaker do well and why?

10. Consider content. What could the speaker do better and why?

Name _____Section _____Date _____

AUDIENCE ASSESSMENT FORM

What type of group was the speaker addressing?

1. Size of group:

2. Is attendance expected or voluntary?

    Expected   Voluntary

3. What are the demographic characteristics that apply to this situation?

    Age:

    Socioeconomic status:

    Race:

    Education and training:

    Sex:

What seems to be the group's attitude toward the topic? Circle the number that best answers the question.

Positive			*Indifferent*		*Negative*	
1	2	3	4	5	6	7

What seems to be the group's attitude toward the speaker? Circle the number that best answers the question.

Positive			*Indifferent*		*Negative*	
1	2	3	4	5	6	7

What does the group already know about the topic?

List the ways in which the speaker is like the group.

List the ways in which the speaker is unlike the group.

PRESENTATIONAL AIDS IN PUBLIC SPEAKING

Presentational aids can serve to **enhance your speech** by:

- Clarifying complex concepts
- Making abstract verbal messages more concrete
- Adding novelty/variety
- Enhancing credibility/persuasive appeal
- Increasing listener retention
- Reducing public speaking anxiety

There are a variety of types of presentational aids, including audiovisual aids (i.e., videotapes), audio aids (i.e., CD's and cassette tapes), and visual aids (usually presented on posters, overhead transparancies, flip charts, computer generated graphics, etc.). Presentational aids can enhance your speech best if you follow certain general guidelines as you construct them and as you integrate them into your public speech.

CONSTRUCTION GUIDELINES

Audio and AudioVisual Aids: If you are using audio or audiovisual aids, be sure your excerpt is short. A 20-second excerpt will seem very long as you are presenting your speech. Strive to limit them to 10–20 seconds each. Usually, time constraints do not allow for use of more than one or two excerpts. Also, edit your tape carefully so you may use it flawlessly during the presentation. Have the tape cued to the exact spot prior to beginning the speech. If you are using more than one excerpt, use two different tapes cued to the right spot or edit one tape in a way the alleviates the neccessity to fast forward.

Visual Aids: Several tips will serve you well as you prepare.

1. Keep them simple. Generally, limit each visual aid to one main point. If you decide to use visual aids to make more than one point, use more than one visual aid. Too much information on one visual aid is confusing and actually distracts from the clarity of the message.

2. Make them large. Make sure the visual aid (and the headings, titles, and verbal descriptions) are large enough to be seen easily in the back of the room where you will be presenting. Visual aids that are too small hurt your credibility and do not serve to embellish the verbal message of your speech.

3. Use primary and bold colors. Avoid pastels. They are difficult to see from the back of the room. Also limit colors on each visual aid to two or three. More colors becomes cluttered and ends up distracting from the message.

4. Prepare them neatly. Feel free to use stencils, computer-generated graphics, a roommate who is an art major is you need help achieving this. Sloppily prepared visual aids do not enhance a speech. They hurt credibility and distract from the verbal message.

5. Use a different symbol system. Too often, students prepare visual aids that simply restate what they are saying in the speech. A list of items or key terms does not make abstract concepts more concrete. To enhance the verbal message, the presentational aid must represent the idea

using a different symbol system (i.e., pictures, diagrams, graphs, charts, and so forth). An ethically prepared presentational aid uses a symbol system *other than just the verbal symbol system* so that it enhances meanings offered verbally in the speech itself.

INTEGRATION GUIDELINES

1. Effective presentational aids are concealed until they are to be referenced in the speech. You will need to practice concealing, disclosing, and concealing again your presentational aids in advance to ensure smooth integration.

2. Effective presentational aids are referred to orally and visually as you are discussing them. They do not stand alone in a public speech. They must be referenced as they are discussed. In doing so, however, take care to remain "open" to your audience by referencing them with the appropriate hand. If your visual aids are displayed on a screen (as in an overhead transparency or PowerPoint visual aids), then be sure to reference the image on the screen where you want your listeners' eyes to be focused. You might need to use a "pointer" for this. If so, remember to remain "open" to your audience.

3. Effective presentational aids are smoothly demonstrated. You can only achieve this by practicing with them as you rehearse your speech in advance.

USING POWERPOINT VISUAL AIDS
STEP-BY-STEP CREATION PROCESS

Pam Zaug, North Dakota State University Graduate Student, Spring 1998

HOW TO BEGIN

Click on Start. Scroll to Programs and click on it once. Scroll to Microsoft Applications for Windows and click on it. Scroll to Microsoft Power Point and click on it once Power Point will open up to a rectangular box with four options: AutoContent Wizard, Template, Blank Presentation, and Open an Existing Presentation.

TEMPLATE

Click on Template. Allows you to pick a template (background, text colors, fonts, bullets....) Once you have picked a template, *click on Apply Design Template.* The template may be changed at any-time, but it will change all of the slides. There should be no reason to change the font size or type within the selected template. The screen and room where Power Point presentation is to be used will affect the type of template used by the speaker.

Template Don'ts:
Pastel Colors or extremely Dark Colors.

Suggested Templates:
In Content File: FINANC 0, FLYER 0, MKTPLN 0, PHOME 0, PRJOVR S, PROG 0, STATUS 0.

Designs File:
CONTEMP, CONTPORT, DADSTIE, HIGHVOLT, NOTEBOOK, PORTNOTE, PROFESS.

The next screen is the New Slide which is a chart of organizational patterns. For now, click on the slide in the upper left corner. This is the slide format to be used for your title slide of presentation.

TOOL BARS

There is a Menu Bar (the top row), Standard Tool Bar (2nd row), Formatting Tool Bar (3rd row), and the Drawing Tool Bar (vertical bar on the left side of the screen). By using the mouse to move the cursor to any icon on any of the bars, will provide a yellow box (Tool Tip) that describes the icon's function.

Go to the Standard Tool Bar and click on the icon that looks like a sparkle, referred to as the New Slide icon. A chart of organizational patterns for slides will appear. Click on any organizational pattern depending on what you need to create for the presentation.

SLIDE VIEWS

Look at the bottom of the screen in the left corner. This is the Slide Views Tool Bar which allows you to look at your slide in many different formats. Click on the first icon in the left corner. This is the Slide View.

The Slide View shows a slide at a time. You can add text, graphs, and charts and see exactly what a slide will look like in your presentation. This view is where most typing will occur.

Now follow the directions on the screen. *Go to the top rectangle, click and type a Title for a presentation.* When finished typing, *click on the bottom box and type your name/group members' names.* When finished it should look like this screen:

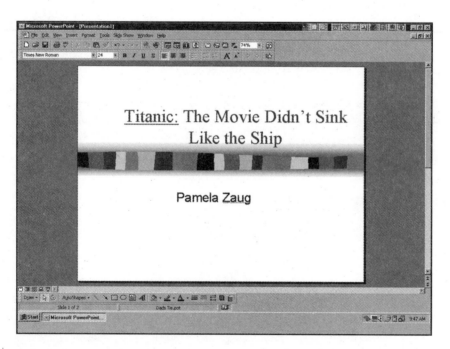

Return to Slide Views Tool Bar and click on the second icon, the Outline View.

Shows an outline of the text on your slides. (No graphics, charts, etc.) Great for an overview of your presentation. Use to reorganize text information. Not as easy as the Slide View to work within.

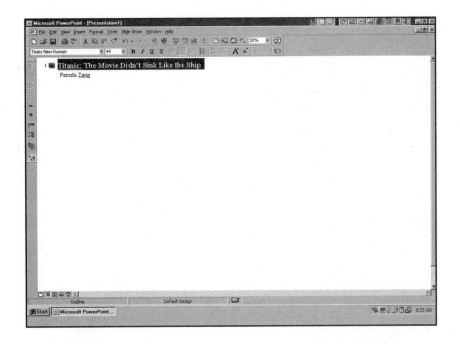

Return to Slide Views Tool Bar and click on the third icon, the Slide Sorter View.

Displays miniatures of each slide. Reorganize your presentation, delete slides, add transitions, builds, and rehearse timings. If you notice the Formatting Tool Bar (3rd tool bar) changes in this view, which will be important for Transitions and Builds.

****Remember that you will be constantly be moving back and forth between slide views while creating your PowerPoint Presentation.

58

Return to Slide Views Tool Bar and click on the fourth icon, the Notes Page View.

Create notes you can print and use during a presentation. The slide is on the top half of the page with your notes on the bottom half. By going to the Standard Tool Bar (2nd row) and clicking on the number with a percent sign, you can change the font size on the notes page.

Return to Slide Views Tool Bar and click on the fifth icon the Slide Show View (presentation view).

Displays your presentation over the entire screen of the computer/projector. A good way to practice the presentation in this view.

CREATING THE SLIDE SHOW

Go to Slide Views Tool Bar. *Click on Slide Sorter View (3rd icon).* Go to Standard Tool Bar (2nd row) and *click on the New Slide icon (sparkle) for organizational formatting. Click on the second format.* Return to Slide Views Tool Bar, *click on Slide View (1st icon).* Using the topic from Title slide pick an aspect of the topic. *Click on the top box and type topic.*

Click on the second box and type subtopics. Hit return after each subtopic. Bullets will appear.

If you want sub-subtopics below each of the subtopics with further indentation, *type the whole list at once. Then next to each sub-subtopic hit tab.*

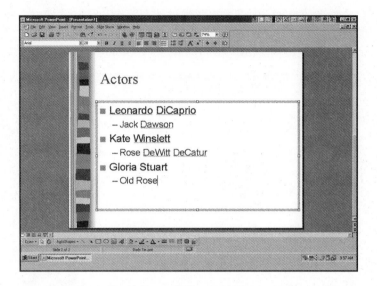

GRAPHS

Return to Slide Views Tool Bar, *click on Slide Sorter View. Click on New Slide* on Standard Tool Bar to create a new slide. *Click on the icon with a graph. Click on Slide View. Click on the Title area and type a title.*

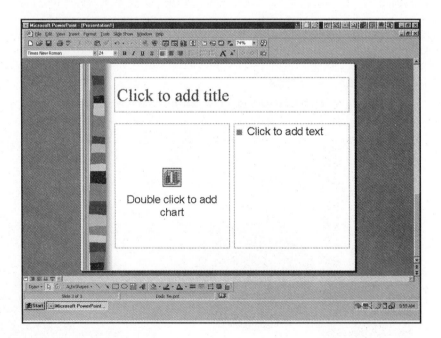

Double-click on the Graph Area. Click on the data sheet to fill in labels for rows and columns and numbers. When in this format, the Main Tool Bar adds a Chart field to pick different types of charts.

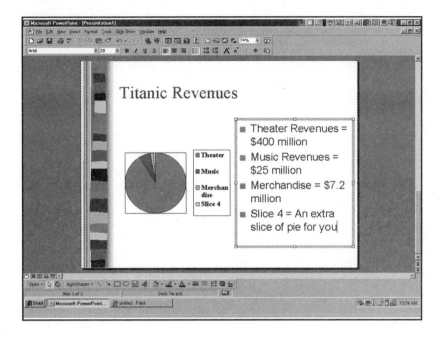

CLIP ART

Click on the Slide Sorter View. Click on New Slide. Click on the square with picture of a man. Click on Slide View. Double Click on the picture/clip art. This allows you to select any type of clip art available. *Scroll up and down the selections. When you find your art click on it. Click on insert.* You can change the size and position of the slide. When the tiny boxes are surrounding the clip art, *click on one of the boxes.* The 4-Way arrow moves the clip art around. The diagonal arrow changes the size of the clip art.

For text click on the other box and type.

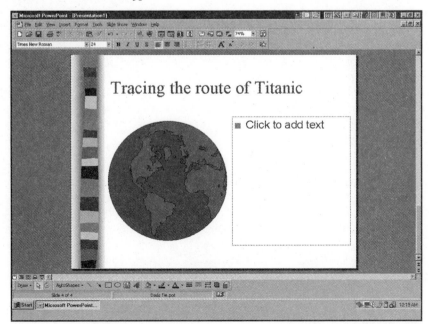

TRANSITIONS

Transitions are used to create the shift from one slide to another. There are many effects to choose from. **Don't use too many different ones, they can be distracting. Consistency is a sign of a professional presentation.**

Click on Slide Sorter View. On the left end of the Formatting Tool Bar (3rd tool bar) where it says No Transition, *click on the left side box or click on the transition arrow on its right side.*

BUILDS

Builds are transitions within a slide. They are effective in slides containing bullets as each bullet can appear on the slide separately by clicking the mouse button. **Remember, when using the visual aids you don't want to show your information until it is necessary in the presentation.**

Click on Slide Sorter View. On the Formatting Tool Bar, to the right of the Transition icon, click on the Builds box where it says No Effect.

EDITING THE PRESENTATION

Deleting Slides: *Click on Slide Sorter View. Click on slide to be deleted.* A dark square should be around the slide. *Hit delete.* If you accidentally delete the wrong slide, *go into Edit and click on Undo Typing.*

Rearranging Slides: *Click on Slide Sorter View. Click on slide to be moved.* A dark square should be around the slide.

Blank Slides: *Click on blank slide between each formatted slide for your presentation.*

SAVING THE PRESENTATION

Place floppy into Disk Drive A. Go to Menu Tool Bar, click on File. Click on Save As... Click on My Documents Down Arrow. Click on 3-1/2 Floppy (A:). Type a name for the presentation. Hit Save.

PRINT OPTIONS

Go to Menu Tool Bar. Click on File. Click on Print. Go to the bottom of the screen where it says Print What. Slides and click on arrow for choices. Print the slides one, two, three, or six to a page. Three is usually the most effective if the audience needs to take notes. Be sure to select black and white unless using a color printer. Try printing one page first. **Remember that technology does not work 100% of the time, so print a hard copy of the slides and transfer them to transparencies to use on an overhead for an emergency situation!!!**

BEGINNING THE PRESENTATION

Click on Start. Scroll to Microsoft PowerPoint and click on It once. Power Point will open up to a rectangular box with four options: AutoContent Wizard, Template, AutoLayouts, and Open an Existing Presentation. *Click on Open an Existing Presentation, Place floppy into Disk Drive. Click on My Computer. Click on 311, Floppy (A:). Click on presentation title. Click on Open.* You should be in Slide Sorter View. Make sure that there is a dark square around your first slide, insuring that the slide show will start in the correct place. *Click on Slide Show View. Hit the letter B to create a Black Screen.* This allows you to return to the *same screen* when you are ready to continue discussing it.

NAVIGATING THE PRESENTATION

Space Bar = Next Slide

Mouse:
    Left Button = Next Slide
    Right Button = Menu

Arrow Keys:
    Down or Right Arrow = Next Slide
    Up or Left Arrow = Previous Slide

Page Keys:
    Page Down = Next Slide
    Page Up = Previous Slide

Home = First Slide

End = Last Slide

Escape Key:
    Takes you out of the presentation at any point,

    Letter B = Black Screen

* Remember, the guidelines for *constructing* and *integrating* visual aids apply for PowerPoint multimedia presentational aids, as well.

INFORMATIVE SPEECHES

Informative speeches are those that impart knowledge to listeners in order to create shared understanding. In this course, you will be asked to prepare and present three informative speeches: the speech of self-introduction, the speech of personal significance, and the speech of information and diversity.

THE SPEECH OF SELF INTRODUCTION

Description: This is a 2- to 3-minute speech introducing yourself to the class. The lectern is not allowed for this speech. An extemporaneous delivery style (using a key word outline) is required. You are to speak from a *speaking outline* using no more than two 3 × 5 inch index cards (one side only). This special speech "to introduce" is actually an opportunity to inform your listeners about yourself. Your objective is to share some aspects of your personal life with your listeners.

Rationale: Since one of the major fears that increases public speaking anxiety in beginning speakers is the "fear of the unknown," this speech allows classmates to begin getting to know one another, thereby reducing public speaking anxiety for the upcoming speeches. This abbreviated speech also employs the public speaking anxiety reduction method of systematic desensitization. Since this speech builds on the "icebreaker" speaking opportunity offered to students on the first day(s) of class, it is essentially a second—slightly more threatening—communication experience. Systematic desensitization suggests that students can reduce anxiety and develop confidence about their public speaking ability by introducing them *incrementally* to more threatening oral communication tasks.

Special Requirements: Your instructor may or may not provide you with specific areas around which to build your main points. For example, you may be asked to talk about (a) your personal background, (b) where you hope to be in five years (personal and professional goals), and (c) something unique about you or your experiences. These three areas, then, would constitute your main points. Whether or not to specify main point themes is at the discretion of each instructor.

GRADING CRITERIA FOR THE SPEECH OF SELF-INTRODUCTION

Public speeches are critiqued and graded based on our ability to perform effectively in terms of (a) delivery, (b) structure, and (c) content. Expectations for each speech become more demanding as the semester progresses. Expectations for this speech are as follows:

■ For this 10 point speech, you will earn a passing grade simply by attempting the performance. In other words, if you make a serious attempt to give this speech, you will earn *6 of the 10 points*. To earn additional points, you must demonstrate specific skills in terms of delivery, structure, and content.

Delivery

Use of Voice: If you can **sound conversational** (like you are *talking with us* rather than reading to us or presenting in front of us), and if you are **intelligible** (using rate, volume, and pitch that make you understandable), you will earn *1 additional point*.

Use of Body: If you can look **poised** (stand firmly on both feet without shifting around, playing with your notes, hair, or pants pockets), and if you can demonstrate good **eye contact** by looking listeners in the eye and spanning the room, you will earn *1 additional point*.

Structure

If you offer an **attention catcher, thesis statement,** and **preview** in your introduction, **transitions** in your body, and a **thesis restatement,** a **summary** and a **clincher** (beyond "thank you") in your conclusion, you will earn *1 additional point*.

Content

If you talk about each of the 2 or 3 areas described by your instructor and do so within the 2- to 3-minute time frame, you will earn *1 additional point*.

SELF-INTRODUCTION SPEECH EXAMPLE

Formal Outline: "Left on a Doorstep"

Cara Langaas

Introduction

I. **Attention Catcher:** Since birth, I've had a unique childhood. As a newborn baby, I was abandoned on a police station doorstep. Enclosed with me was a note left from my birth mother. My life began in an orphanage in Seoul, South Korea. I lived there for five months where I was fed five times daily by a bottle propped up with a sponge.

II. **Listener Relevance Link:** Although my life began in an unusual manner, you might be surprised as to how much you all and I have in common.

III. **Thesis Statement:** I'm Cara Langaas, and I'd like to introduce myself to you today by sharing some of the experiences I've been through as they have shaped who I am today.

IV. **Preview:** I'll talk about my childhood adoption experience, my passion for sports, and my goals for the future.

Transition: My unusual childhood was the start of my unique life.

Body

I. **First Main Point:** Things really began to fall into place when I was put up for adoption, which you all may feel was a bit unorthodox for a child to go through. (**Listener Relevance**)

   A. **Subpoint:** I was adopted by a young couple who lived in Greenbush, Minnesota, a small town just south of Canada. When my parents divorced, my brother and I moved to Thief River Falls with my mom. While my mom worked and went to college, we lived in a shambled two-bedroom home that lacked decent heat during the cold Minnesota winters.

   B. **Subpoint:** While trying to support my older brother and me, my mother met her future husband. His job brought the four of us to Eagan, Minnesota, a suburb of the Twin Cities. After a few years, we moved to a nice neighborhood in Rosemount. That's where we remain today. After a lot of hard work, my stepfather became President and C.E.O. for a chain of massage schools and clinics in Minnesota and North Dakota.

Transition: My early childhood was very unique and sometimes I still wonder if I would have been as active in sports if I had remained in that small town in Northern Minnesota.

II. **Second Main Point:** As a child I really began to develop my love for sports.

   Listener Relevance: You all probably tried a sport at some point in your lives.

   A. **Subpoint:** I tried to play every sport possible. I began playing soccer when I was in the fifth grade. I went on to play soccer, basketball, softball, track, and golf for Rosemount High School. I also participated in year round soccer leagues, recreational hockey, karate, dance, and even coached my little brother's soccer team, as well as worked as my school's assistant athletic trainer.

B. **Subpoint:** I was so busy with sports that I barely found time to do my other favorite things: hang out with my friends and shop.

C. **Subpoint:** When I wasn't participating in sports, hanging with my friends, or shopping, I worked at *Play It Again Sports*.

Transition: As you can see, sports has become an important part of my leisure time and my work time. I hope that my interest for sports continues to be an important part of my life in the future.

III. **Third Main Point:** Just dreaming of the goals I have for the future excites me.

Listener Relevance: Every student often visualizes the life they intend for their future.

A. **Subpoint:** I plan to graduate from NDSU as a certified secondary education teacher. I hope to become a high school biology teacher for a suburban high school.

B. **Subpoint:** I also hope to coach soccer for the high school where I am employed. I love working with children and athletes, and really hope to do both.

Conclusion

I. **Thesis restatement:** So, now you understand how all my experiences have kept my life full of excitement and shaped who I am today.

II. **Main point summary:** My childhood adoption experiences, my love for sports, and my future goals all contribute to my character.

III. **Clincher:** It might sound odd, but I am actually grateful for being left on that police station doorstep. It was the first of many experiences that have shaped my life and who I am today.

Name _____ Section _____

Title of Speech

PREPARATION OUTLINE: SPEECH OF SELF-INTRODUCTION

Introduction

I.   Attention Catcher:

II. Thesis Statement:

III. Preview:

Body

I.   First Main Point:

    A.

    B.

   Transition:

II. Second Main Point:

    A.

    B.

   Transition:

III. Third Main Point:

    A.

    B.

Conclusion

I.   Thesis restatement:

II. Main point summary:

III. Clincher:

Name _____   Section _____

INSTRUCTOR CRITIQUE FORM:
SPEECH OF SELF-INTRODUCTION

(10 points)

ASPECT	CRITIQUE
Delivery *Voice:* Conversational? Intelligible?	
Body: Eye Contact? Poise? (Swaying, fidgeting, etc.) Attire?	
Structure Attention Catcher? Thesis Statement? Preview? Transitions? Thesis Restatement? Summary of Main Points? Clincher?	
Content All main points addressed? Supporting material included? Met time constraint?	

Total Points:

Name _____ Section _____

SELF-CRITIQUE FORM:

SPEECH OF SELF-INTRODUCTION

Goal: To evaluate your own performance.

Rationale: As a form of cognitive restructuring, this exercise can help reduce public speaking anxiety while it helps you improve as a public speaker.

Directions: **(a)** In groups of four to six students, discuss your last speech performance based on the following guidelines. Then, complete and turn in this form based on your thoughts and the group discussion. OR **(b)** Watch a videotape of yourself giving your last speech. Complete this form and turn it in.

1. In terms of **Delivery,** the requirements for this speech were to sound intelligible, conversational, and sincere; and to look poised and use effective eye contact. I did the following things well in my last speech:

a.

b.

2. In terms of **Content,** the requirements were to talk about each of the main points and do so within the time constraint. I did the following things well in my last speech:

a.

b.

3. In terms of **Structure,** the requirements were to offer an attention catcher, thesis statement, preview, transitions, thesis restatement, summary, and clincher (beyond "thank you"). I did the following things well in my last speech:

a.

b.

4. If I could do my last speech over again, I would do the following things differently:

a.

b.

c.

5. Overall, I would give myself a grade of _____ on my last speech because....

6. To improve as a public speaker on my next speech, I am going to try to:

a.

b.

THE SPEECH OF PERSONAL SIGNIFICANCE

Description: This is a 4- to 6-minute speech informing us about an object, a person, an event, or a belief that has helped to shape who you are today. Main points should be specific characteristics or values that you hold. These characteristics or values are somehow represented by your object, person, event, or belief. Supporting material for each main point must come from personal life experiences. Listeners should come away knowing *why* this person, object, event, or belief is important to you. The lectern is not allowed for this speech. An extemporaneous delivery style (using a key word outline) is required. Points will be deducted for going over or under the time limits, for not using a *speaking outline*, (key words and phrases, or for using more than five 3 x 5 inch index cards (one side only).

Rationale: There are two primary reasons for requiring this speech. First, beginning speakers sometimes fail to realize that supporting material (evidence) can come from personal experiences, as well as from library research. This speech requires them to draw upon their own experiences and the experiences of real people whom they know. Second, this speech is grounded in the self-disclosure research that suggests that communication anxiety decreases when participants feel as though they are speaking to people whom they know (rather than strangers). This speech is designed to reduce communication anxiety through self-disclosure.

Special Requirements: Each individual instructor may or may not specify particular requirements for speakers enrolled in their section(s).

GRADING CRITERIA
THE SPEECH OF PERSONAL SIGNIFICANCE

Delivery

Use of Voice:

- You need to be intelligible (understood). For this to occur, your rate and your volume need to be appropriate. You need to use clear enunciation and pronunciation.
- You need to be conversational. In other words, it needs to sound like you are talking with us rather than presenting in front of us or reading to us. You need to sound like you are communicating ideas. (Extemporaneous delivery: Key Word Outline)
- You need to sound sincere as you speak. In terms of vocal variety and emotion, you simply need to sound like this is really how you feel.

Use of Body:

- Attire: To convey ethos (competence and credibility), you need to dress up a bit more formally than your listeners.
- Poise: You need to show no distracting nonverbal cues (i.e., shifting, swaying, playing with notes, etc.). Listeners should not be visually distracted from the message by your mannerisms.
- Eye Contact: You need to look listeners in the eyes, span the entire room, and look up from your notes at least 90% of the time. (Extemp: Key Word Outline)

Structure

Macrostructure:

- All elements of the outline must be clearly articulated without needing to refer to the formal typed outline. Transitions must verbally tie the two points together.

Microstructure:

- Your language needs to be inclusive ("we" language and politically correct) and concrete (we should not need a dictionary to look up definitions of the words you use).
- "Verbal garbage" (vocalized pauses like "um," "uh," "like," and "ya know") should be kept to a minimum. Too many tend to distract listeners from the message.
- No slang
- Technical jargon should be defined the first time it is used.

Content

Analysis/Reasoning:

- Your main points should describe characteristics or values that might be universally shared.
- Your content should be descriptive and personally significant.
- You need to be within the time constraint.

Supporting Material

- Your supporting material should come from personal life experiences.
- Your examples should help listeners realize why you picked the main point you picked.

PERSONAL SIGNIFICANCE SPEECH OUTLINE EXAMPLE

Formal Outline: "My Aunt Barb"

Denelle Wolff

Introduction

I. **Attention Catcher:** When I was younger, my favorite bedtime story was *Charlie and the Chocolate Factory*. Every night and sometimes during the day I would beg my parents to read it to me. Needless to say, they grew tired of *Charlie and the Chocolate Factory* and insisted on reading me different stories. The one person I could count on to never stop reading my favorite story was my Aunt Barb. I could count on her to read me *Charlie and the Chocolate Factory* with the same energy and enthusiasm as she did the first time.

II. **Listener Relevance:** The people who affect us as children also shape our lives as adults—this is true for everyone.

III. **Speaker Credibility:** I have spent many years with my Aunt Barb and have learned so much about her life and her contributions to my life.

IV. **Thesis Statement:** My Aunt Barb has had a great impact on my life and helped me become who I am today.

V. **Preview:** The many *gifts* she gave me while growing up serve as reminders of two important lessons she taught me-how to always be *honest* and how not to be afraid *to be my own person*.

Body

I. **First Main Point:** My Aunt Barb always gave me the most creative gifts.

  A. **Subpoint:** She gave me a quilt stitched together from my baby clothes.

    1. **Sub-Subpoint:** Clothes are from infancy to about five years old.

    2. **Sub-Subpoint:** Whenever I look at the quilt, I am reminded of myself.

    3. **Sub-Subpoint:** I am also reminded of all the hard work and time my Aunt Barb devoted to making the quilt for me.

  B. **Subpoint:** One Christmas, Aunt Barb gave me a hand-knit sweater.

    1. **Sub-Subpoint:** I remember being so happy because of all the work she put into it, truly making it a part of her.

    2. **Sub-Subpoint:** Because of the sweater, I will always remember my Aunt Barb.

Transition: These gifts serve as reminders of all the special qualities such as honesty and being true to oneself that Barb brought to my life.

II. **Second Main Point:** Barb taught me about honesty.

  A. **Subpoint:** My Aunt Barb lives an untraditional lifestyle.

    1. **Sub-Subpoint:** Barb could have lied about her lifestyle to make it easier on the people around her.

2. **Sub-Subpoint:** Barb was always open and honest about who she was and the way she wanted to live.

3. **Sub-Subpoint:** I am thankful for my Aunt Barb because she taught me to be honest in what I do.

B. **Subpoint:** Barb was always honest about her past mistakes.

1. **Sub-Subpoint:** Barb never cared to be a role model.

2. **Sub-Subpoint:** Barb always admitted when she did things wrong, she took responsibility for her own actions.

3. **Sub-Subpoint:** I now try to do this myself in my own life.

Transition: Barb was also honest about her right to be her own person.

III. **Third Main Point:** She believed in being her own person.

A. **Subpoint:** My aunt is a lesbian and has been living with the same life partner for as long as I can remember.

B. **Subpoint:** Living this kind of lifestyle was harder to do in the past because people weren't as accepting of it as they are now.

1. **Sub-Subpoint:** She did it strongly and with confidence.

2. **Sub-Subpoint:** She taught me that I don't need to worry about what other people think of me—I live the life I want to lead.

Transition: These are only some of the important qualities that my Aunt Barb gave to me.

Conclusion

I. **Thesis restatement :** Barb shaped my life and I see parts of her in who I am today.

II. **Main point summary:** Whenever I look at the gifts she gave me as a child, I am reminded of her honesty and of her being her own person.

III. **Clincher:** I only hope that my children are as fortunate to be able to sit on Aunt Barb's lap and hear the story of *Charlie and the Chocolate Factory.*

PERSONAL SIGNIFICANCE SPEECH OUTLINE EXAMPLE

Formal Outline: "Anatomy of a Hate Crime"

Chuck Lindstrom

Introduction

I. **Attention Catcher:** Murder. Simply the word itself can send chills through your body, but what if the only reason you were killed was because of something you had no control over? That's where the term *hate crime* comes in. A hate crime is defined as "the violence of intolerance and bigotry, intended to hurt and intimidate someone because of their race, ethnicity, national origin, religion, sexual orientation, or disability" according to *Community Relations Service (1997)*.

II. **Listener Relevance:** Even if we ourselves are never a victim of a hate crime, it is an important issue we can all learn something from.

III. **Speaker Credibility:** I have had a friend fall victim to a hate crime, and my experiences have inspired me to talk about this issue with you today.

IV. **Thesis Statement:** In the next few minutes, let's discuss why the story of Matthew Shepard, portrayed in the film "Anatomy of a Hate Crime," is significant to me.

V. **Preview:** To do so, I'll begin by describing some of the events of the film. Second, let's explore how these events compare to real life. And finally, let's consider how pervasive this issue really is.

Body

I. **First Main Point:** The difference between Matthew Shepard and us is that he experienced more hate in his lifetime than most of us will in ours.

    A. **Subpoint:** Because of his parents' careers, Matthew moved around the world a lot, constantly learning and experiencing new and different things.

        1. **Sub-subpoint:** He grew up in a small town, which teaches a person how to be independent but blind to the real world. I know this from personal experience as well.

        2. **Sub-subpoint:** After living in Saudi Arabia and then Denver, he decided to move to the small town of Laramie, Wyoming, to attend college.

    B. **Subpoint:** Matthew had no idea what was about to happen to him that night on October 6, 1998.

        1. **Sub-subpoint:** After learning he received a good score on one of his midterm exams, he decided to go out to the local bar to celebrate. Two homophobic young men had different plans for him.

        2. **Sub-subpoint:** They offered to give Matthew a ride home, to which he agreed. During the ride home, the two men began beating Matthew to rob him and the events got out of hand. The two men eventually beat Matthew and left him tied to a fence out of town. He was found the next morning and died after 6 days in intensive care.

Transition: This story disgusts and disturbs me and let me tell you why.

II. **Second Main Point:** This story made me so sick and let me tell you why.

    A. **Subpoint:** I hadn't realized how ignorant I had been about understanding the true meaning of hate crimes.

        1. **Sub-subpoint:** I never had fully understood what a hate crime is.

        2. **Sub-subpoint:** According to the Human Rights Campaign (1998), hate crimes have risen 59% from 1991–1998.

        3. **Sub-subpoint:** I had no clue as to how many people are victims of hate crime.

    B. **Subpoint:** After the film, I became much more aware of hate crimes.

        1. **Sub-subpoint:** I am much more sensitive and understanding of people's beliefs and lifestyles.

        2. **Sub-subpoint:** I can now understand how devastating the impact of a hate crime can be.

Transition: Hate crimes are a reality in our nation; crimes that affect us all.

III. **Third Main Point:** In my opinion, the issue of hate crimes is very important. In fact, the issue of hate crimes will affect all of us somehow.

    A. **Subpoint:** Let me tell you how pervasive the problem really is.

        1. **Sub-subpoint:** A hate crime, on average, will occur approximately every 5 hours of each day, in the U.S. alone. (*1998 Hate Crime Statistics*, Human Rights Campaign)

        2. **Sub-subpoint:** Think about how often it occurs around the world.

        3. **Sub-subpoint:** Who in this room has been a victim or has known someone?

        4. **Sub-subpoint:** Hate crimes can happen to anyone for many reasons. For example, let's say Amy here is among a predominately black group of people, and is physically persecuted solely for the color of her skin. Now, she's done nothing wrong, but because of what race she is, she becomes a victim.

        5. **Sub-subpoint:** The Holocaust was one big hate crime.

    B. **Subpoint:** Legislation is currently being discussed and passed in nearly all state governments.

        1. **Sub-subpoint:** Only seven states have no hate crime law in place.

        2. **Sub-subpoint:** Wyoming is one of those states, even after the Matthew Shepard incident.

Transition: Hate crimes have significantly affected the person I am today.

Conclusion

I. **Thesis restatement:** So now I have explained why the film, "Anatomy of a Hate Crime" is significant to me.

II. **Main point summary:** We have discussed the tragic story of Matthew Shepard, why that story disgusts me, and how pervasive hate crimes really are.

III. **Clincher:** Maybe with hope, future generations won't need to know the definition of a hate crime. I only wish that being gay myself didn't put me at so much risk as it does today.

References

Human Rights Campaign. (2000, December 18). 1998 Hate Crime Statistics [4 graphs]. *Human Rights Campaign* [Online]. Available at: http://www.hrc.org/issues/hate/stats98.html (version on January 31, 2001).

Human Rights Campaign. (2000, December 18). Community Relations Service [12 paragraphs]. *Human Rights Campaign* [Online]. Available at: http://www.hrc.org/issues/hate/ (version on January 31, 2001).

PERSONAL SIGNIFICANCE SPEECH OUTLINE EXAMPLE

Formal Outline: "Find a Penny Pick it Up"

Michelle Zentz

Introduction

I. **Attention Catcher:** Find a penny pick it up and all day long you'll have good luck. A penny for your thoughts. Watch your pennies and your dollars will take care of themselves. A penny saved is a penny earned.

II. **Listener Relevance:** Many of you probably have heard these expressions. But, would any of you bother to pick up a penny? Maybe not, but pennies can add up.

III. **Speaker Credibility:** I know they do. Pennies have and do represent more to me than just one cent.

IV. **Thesis Statement:** Today, I am going to tell you how the penny has been significant in my life.

V. **Preview:** Specifically, I will tell you the role pennies have played during my childhood, my teenage years, and the role that pennies have played recently during my adulthood.

Transition: So how was the penny significant in my childhood?

Body

I. **First Main Point:** My childhood duties helping my Dad helped me discover the value of a penny at a young age.

　A. **Subpoint:** My Dad owned a bar. It was the job of my sister and I to sort through the pennies in the till to find the wheat pennies that Dad collected. For our efforts, we were allowed to keep the rest of the pennies. Those pennies in my childhood meant penny candy. Black Jack taffy was my favorite. Red coins and sixlets were only two for a penny.

　B. **Subpoint:** But I developed diabetes and could no longer spend my money on candy. My sister taught me how to roll them in papers so they could be deposited in the bank. After my sister graduated, I didn't have to share the precious coins and the pennies added up quickly. As a small child, those pennies meant candy. As I grew, those pennies taught me about counting, sharing, and managing money.

Transition: Now that I have told you how pennies were important in my childhood, I will tell you how they were important in my teenage years.

II. **Second Main Point:** Those pennies I collected helped me realize my teenage dreams of travel.

　A. **Subpoint:** At age 14, 1 went to Washington D.C. with my 4-H group. The pennies I had saved in childhood served as spending money while I was on the trip. While in Washington, I saw many attractions, but it was the Lincoln Memorial that made the greatest impact on me. Yes, the very same monument featured on the back of the very important penny.

B. **Subpoint:** I was shocked by the size of the Lincoln Memorial. It was much larger than the one on the back of the penny! Flood lights shone on pillars of alabaster, and it was taller than anything I'd every seen before. The copper colored statue of Lincoln was so large that his shoe was taller than I was. I felt like I was in a sacred place. This attraction was my favorite of the week-long trip. The lesson I learned was that those pennies saved helped me to fulfill my dream of travel.

Transition: Now that I have told you how pennies were important in my teenage years, I will tell you how they were important in my recent adulthood.

III. **Third Main Point:** Pennies remained important in my adulthood but for a different reason.

A. **Subpoint:** At a retreat for blind adults at Camp Grassick last summer, I participated in a class for communication skills. The class instructor held a competition. She gave pennies to certain campers. The only way a student could get a coin was to strike up a conversation and shake their hand. I greeted everyone at the entire camp and received a prize for meeting the most people.

B. **Subpoint:** I was excited to win but the joke was on me! The award was a gag fake rubber hand. But, the penny contest helped me step out of the circle of friends I had made in prior years. The penny, in my adulthood, helped me to meet some new and interesting friends.

Transition: So, the penny represents more to me than a copper coin or a minute amount of money.

Conclusion

I. **Thesis restatement:** Today, I told you how the penny has been significant in my life.

II. **Main point summary:** Specifically, I told you the role pennies have played during my childhood, my teenage years, and the role that pennies have played recently during my adulthood.

III. **Clincher:** So, find a penny pick it up and all day long you will have good luck. Watch your pennies and your dollars will take care of themselves. A penny saved truly is a penny earned. A penny for your thoughts . . . have you ever thought of the penny as being significant

Name: _____ Section: _____

Title of Speech: _____

PREPARATION OUTLINE:
THE SPEECH OF PERSONAL SIGNIFICANCE

Introduction

I.   Attention Catcher:

II. Listener Relevance Link:

III. Speaker Credibility:

IV. Thesis Statement:

V.   Preview:

Body

1.   First Main Point:

    A. Subpoint:

        1. Sub-subpoint:

        2. Sub-subpoint:

    B. Supporting Point:

        1. Sub-subpoint:

        2. Sub-subpoint:

Transition:

II. Second Main Point:

    A. Subpoint:

        1. Sub-subpoint:

        2. Sub-subpoint:

    B. Subpoint:

        1. Sub-subpoint:

        2. Sub-subpoint:

Transition:

III. Third Main Point:

    A. Subpoint:

        1. Sub-subpoint:

        2. Sub-subpoint:

    B. Subpoint:

       1. Sub-subpoint:

       2. Sub-subpoint:

Transition:

Conclusion

I.   Thesis restatement:

II. Main point summary:

III. Clincher:

Name: _____   Section: _____

Title of Speech: _____

INSTRUCTOR CRITIQUE FORM
THE SPEECH OF PERSONAL SIGNIFICANCE

Rating Scale   7   6   5   4   3   2   1
                (Excellent)   (Poor)

Delivery	Critique	Points
Use of Voice: Intelligibility (rate, volume, pitch, quality, enunciation, pronunciation)? Conversational style? Fluency? Emotional expression (sincerity)?		
Use of Body: Attire? Poise (no distracting cues)? Eye contact?		

Structure		
Macrostructure: Attention catcher? Listener Relevance? Speaker Credibility? Thesis statement? Preview? Transitions? Thesis restatement? Summary of main points? Clincher?		
Microstructure: Language (clear, inclusive)? Technical jargon defined? Slang? Vocalized pauses (verbal garbage—"uh," "um," "like," "ya' know")?		

Content		
Analysis: Supporting points (accurate, varied, depth, related to thesis)? Appropriate focus (time constraint)? Personally significant?		
Supporting Material: Relevant? Distributed throughout? Personal experiences?		

Total Points: _____

Critic (your name): _____ Section: _____

Speaker (person you critiqued): _____

CLASSMATE CRITIQUE FORM
THE SPEECH OF PERSONAL SIGNIFICANCE

Delivery	CRITIQUE (Identify something the speaker did well and why. Identify something the speaker could do to improve, why, and how.)
Use of Voice: Intelligibility (rate, volume, pitch, quality, enunciation, pronunciation)? Conversational style? Emotional expression (sincerity)?	
Use of Body: Attire? Poise (no distracting cues)? Eye contact?	

Structure	CRITIQUE (Identify something the speaker did well and why. Identify something the speaker could do to improve, why, and how.)
Macrostructure: Attention catcher? Listener Relevance? Speaker Credibility? Thesis statement? Preview? Transitions? Thesis restatement? Summary of main points? Clincher?	
Microstructure: Language (clear, inclusive)? Technical jargon defined? No Slang? No vocalized pauses?	

Content	CRITIQUE (Identify something the speaker did well and why. Identify something the speaker could do to improve, why, and how.)
Analysis: Supporting points (appropriate, thematic, breadth, depth, listener relevance)? Appropriate focus (time limit)? Personally significant?	
Supporting Material: Relevant? Personal experiences?	

Critic (your name): _____ Section: _____

Speaker (person you critiqued): _____

CLASSMATE CRITIQUE FORM
THE SPEECH OF PERSONAL SIGNIFICANCE

Delivery	**CRITIQUE** (Identify something the speaker did well and why. Identify something the speaker could do to improve, why, and how.)
Use of Voice: Intelligibility (rate, volume, pitch, quality, enunciation, pronunciation)? Conversational style? Emotional expression (sincerity)?	
Use of Body: Attire? Poise (no distracting cues)? Eye contact?	

Structure	**CRITIQUE** (Identify something the speaker did well and why. Identify something the speaker could do to improve, why, and how.)
Macrostructure: Attention catcher? Listener Relevance? Speaker Credibility? Thesis statement? Preview? Transitions? Thesis restatement? Summary of main points? Clincher?	
Microstructure: Language (clear, inclusive)? Technical jargon defined? No Slang? No vocalized pauses?	

Content	**CRITIQUE** (Identify something the speaker did well and why. Identify something the speaker could do to improve, why, and how.)
Analysis: Supporting points (accurate, varied, depth, related to thesis)? Appropriate focus (time constraint)? Listener Relevance?	
Supporting Material: Relevant? Distributed throughout? Personally significant?	

Name:_____Section:_____

SELF-CRITIQUE FORM:
THE SPEECH OF PERSONAL SIGNIFICANCE

Goal: To evaluate your own performance.

Rationale: As a form of cognitive restructuring, this exercise can help reduce public speaking anxiety while it helps you improve as a public speaker.

Directions: (a) In groups of 4 to 6 students, discuss your last speech performance based on the following guidelines. Then, complete and turn in this form based on your thoughts and the group discussion. OR **(b)** Watch a videotape of yourself giving your last speech. Complete this form and turn it in.

1. In terms of **Delivery,** the requirements for this speech were to sound intelligible, conversational, and sincere; and to look poised, wear appropriate attire, and use effective eye contact. I did the following things well in my last speech:

a.

b.

2. In terms of **Content,** the requirements were to be within the time constraint, offer personal examples, and convey personal significance. I did the following things well in my last speech:

a.

b.

3. In terms of **Structure,** the requirements were to offer all macrostructural elements, use clear and inclusive language, no slang, and no verbal garbage. I did the following things well in my last speech:

a.

b.

4. If I could do my last speech over again, I would do the following things differently:

a.

b.

c.

5. Overall, I would give myself a grade of _____ on my last speech because....

6. To improve as a public speaker on my next speech, I am going to try to:

a.

b.

THE SPEECH OF DEMONSTRATION

Description:

This is a 4- to 6-minute informative speech clarifying a process or procedure in the minds of your listeners. Main points should be arranged chronologically as steps in a sequence. Supporting material should include definitions, explanations, and examples. Listeners should come away knowing how a process or procedure works. The lectern is not allowed for this speech. Points will be deducted for going over or under the time limits, for not using a *speaking outline* (key words and phrases), or for using more than five 3 x 5 inch index cards (one side only).

Rationale:

This is a fairly simple speech for beginning students to prepare and present. As such, they are able to learn to employ the basic elements of speech structure to a fairly non-threatening speech (on a topic about which they are fairly familiar).

GRADING CRITERIA
THE SPEECH OF DEMONSTRATION

Delivery

Use of Voice:

- You need to be intelligible (understood). For this to occur, your rate and your volume need to be appropriate. You need to use clear enunciation and pronunciation.
- You need to be conversational. In other words, it needs to sound like you are talking with us rather than presenting in front of us or reading to us. You need to sound like you are communicating ideas. (Extemporaneous delivery: Key Word Outline)
- You need to sound sincere as you speak. In terms of vocal variety and emotion, you simply need to sound like this is really how you feel.

Use of Body:

- Attire: To convey ethos (competence and credibility), you need to dress up a bit more formally than your listeners.
- Poise: You need to show no distracting nonverbal cues (i.e., shifting, swaying, playing with notes, etc.). Listeners should not be visually distracted from the message by your mannerisms.
- Eye Contact: You need to look listeners in the eyes, span the entire room, and look up from your notes at least 90% of the time.

Structure

Macrostructure:

- All elements of the outline must be clearly articulated without needing to refer to the formal typed outline. Transitions must verbally tie the two points together.

Microstructure:

- Your language needs to be inclusive ("we" language and politically correct) and concrete (we should not need a dictionary to look up definitions of the words you use).
- "Verbal garbage" (vocalized pauses like "um," "uh," "like," and "ya know") should be kept to a minimum. Too many tend to distract listeners from the message.
- No slang
- Technical jargon should be defined the first time it is used.

Content

Analysis/Reasoning:

- Your main points should describe steps in the process or procedure.
- Your content should be descriptive.
- You need to be within the time constraint.

Supporting Material

- Your supporting material should include definitions, explanations, and examples.

Name: _____ Section: _____

Title of Speech: _____

PREPARATION OUTLINE:
THE SPEECH OF DEMONSTRATION

Introduction

I. Attention Catcher:

II. Listener Relevance Link:

III. Speaker Credibility:

IV. Thesis Statement:

V. Preview:

Body

1. First Main Point:

   A. Subpoint:

     1. Sub-subpoint:

     2. Sub-subpoint:

   B. Supporting Point:

     1. Sub-subpoint:

     2. Sub-subpoint:

Transition:

II. Second Main Point:

   A. Subpoint:

     1. Sub-subpoint:

     2. Sub-subpoint:

   B. Subpoint:

     1. Sub-subpoint:

     2. Sub-subpoint:

Transition:

III. Third Main Point:

   A. Subpoint:

     1. Sub-subpoint:

     2. Sub-subpoint:

      B. Subpoint:

          1. Sub-subpoint:

          2. Sub-subpoint:

Transition:

Conclusion

I.   Thesis restatement:

II. Main point summary:

III. Clincher:

Name: _____ Section: _____

Title of Speech: _____

INSTRUCTOR CRITIQUE FORM
THE SPEECH OF DEMONSTRATION

Rating Scale   7   6   5   4   3   2   1
               (Excellent)   (Poor)

Delivery	**Critique**	**Points**
Use of Voice: Intelligibility (rate, volume, pitch, quality, enunciation, pronunciation)? Conversational style? Emotional expression (sincerity)?		
Use of Body: Attire? Poise (no distracting cues)? Eye contact?		

Structure		
Macrostructure: Attention catcher? Listener Relevance? Speaker Credibility? Thesis statement? Preview? Transitions? Thesis restatement? Summary of main points? Clincher?		
Microstructure: Language (clear, inclusive)? Technical jargon defined? Slang? Vocalized pauses (verbal garbage—"uh," "um," "like," "ya' know")?		

Content		
Analysis: Main points (steps in a process or procedure)? Appropriate focus (time constraint)? Listener Relevance?		
Supporting Material: Relevant? Distributed throughout? Definitions, examples, explanations?		

Total Points: _____

Critic (your name): _____ Section: _____

Speaker (person you critiqued): _____

CLASSMATE CRITIQUE FORM
THE SPEECH OF DEMONSTRATION

Delivery	CRITIQUE (Identify something the speaker did well and why. Identify something the speaker could do to improve, why, and how.)
Use of Voice: Intelligibility (rate, volume, pitch, quality, enunciation, pronunciation)? Conversational style? Emotional expression (sincerity)?	
Use of Body: Attire? Poise (no distracting cues)? Eye contact?	

Structure	CRITIQUE (Identify something the speaker did well and why. Identify something the speaker could do to improve, why, and how.)
Macrostructure: Attention catcher? Listener Relevance? Speaker Credibility? Thesis statement? Preview? Transitions? Thesis restatement? Summary of main points? Clincher?	
Microstructure: Language (clear, inclusive)? Technical jargon defined? No Slang? No vocalized pauses?	

Content	CRITIQUE (Identify something the speaker did well and why. Identify something the speaker could do to improve, why, and how.)
Analysis: Main points (steps in a process or procedure)? Appropriate focus (time constraint)? Listener Relevance?	
Supporting Material: Relevant? Distributed throughout? Definitions, explanations, and examples?	

Name:_____Section:_____

SELF-CRITIQUE FORM:
THE SPEECH OF DEMONSTRATION

Goal: To evaluate your own performance.

Rationale: As a form of cognitive restructuring, this exercise can help reduce public speaking anxiety while it helps you improve as a public speaker.

Directions: (a) In groups of 4 to 6 students, discuss your last speech performance based on the following guidelines. Then, complete and turn in this form based on your thoughts and the group discussion. OR (b) Watch a videotape of yourself giving your last speech. Complete this form and turn it in.

1. In terms of Delivery, the requirements for this speech were to sound intelligible, conversational, and sincere; and to look poised, wear appropriate attire, and use effective eye contact. I did the following things well in my last speech:

   a.

   b.

2. In terms of Content, the requirements were to be within the time constraint, offer main points that are steps in the process or procedure, and use definitions, explanations, and examples. I did the following things well in my last speech:

   a.

   b.

3. In terms of Structure, the requirements were to offer all macrostructural elements, use clear and inclusive language, no slang, and no verbal garbage. I did the following things well in my last speech:

   a.

   b.

4. If I could do my last speech over again, I would do the following things differently:

   a.

   b.

   c.

5. Overall, I would give myself a grade of _____ on my last speech because . . . .

6. To improve as a public speaker on my next speech, I am going to try to:

   a.

   b.

THE SPEECH OF NARRATION

Description:
This is a 4- to 6-minute informative speech sharing an interesting, entertaining, or inspirational story. This may be about an event that shaped your life or something you heard or read about. It should be designed to illustrate a moral. Supporting material should include personal experiences (your own or from those individuals in your story), examples, and explanations. Listeners should come away knowing the moral of the story. The lectern is not allowed for this speech. Points will be deducted for going over or under the time limits, for not using a speaking outline (key words and phrases), or for using more than five 3 x 5 inch index cards (one side only).

Rationale:
This is a fairly simple speech for beginning students to prepare and present. As such, they are able to learn to employ the basic elements of speech structure to a fairly non-threatening speech. Also, since students are likely to draw from personal experiences, classmates will get to know one another and, consequently, reduce public speaking anxiety that results from a fear of the unknown.

Special Requirements:
Each individual instructor may or may not specify particular requirements for speakers enrolled in their sections(s).

GRADING CRITERIA
THE SPEECH OF NARRATION

Delivery

Use of Voice:

- You need to be intelligible (understood). For this to occur, your rate and your volume need to be appropriate. You need to use clear enunciation and pronunciation.
- You need to be conversational. In other words, it needs to sound like you are talking with us rather than presenting in front of us or reading to us. You need to sound like you are communicating ideas. (Extemporaneous delivery: Key Word Outline)
- You need to sound sincere as you speak. In terms of vocal variety and emotion, you simply need to sound like this is really how you feel.

Use of Body:

- Attire: To convey ethos (competence and credibility), you need to dress up a bit more formally than your listeners.
- Poise: You need to show no distracting nonverbal cues (i.e., shifting, swaying, playing with notes, etc.). Listeners should not be visually distracted from the message by your mannerisms.
- Eye Contact: You need to look listeners in the eyes, scan the entire room, and look up from your notes at least 90% of the time.

Structure

Macrostructure:

- All elements of the outline must be clearly articulated without needing to refer to the formal typed outline. Transitions must verbally tie the two points together.

Microstructure:

- Your language needs to be inclusive ("we" language and politically correct) and concrete (we should not need a dictionary to look up definitions of the words you use).
- "Verbal garbage" (vocalized pauses like "um," "uh," "like," and "ya know") should be kept to a minimum. Too many tend to distract listeners from the message.
- No slang
- Technical jargon should be defined the first time it is used.

Content

Analysis/Reasoning:

- Your speech should illustrate a moral.
- Your content should be about an event that shaped your life or that your heard or read about that made an impact on your life.
- You need to be within the time constraint.

Supporting Material

- Your supporting material should include personal experiences, definitions, explanations, and examples.

Name _____ Section _____

Title of Speech _____

PREPARATION OUTLINE:
THE SPEECH OF NARRATION

Introduction

I.   Attention Catcher:

II. Listener Relevance Link:

III. Speaker Credibility:

IV. Thesis Statement:

V.   Preview:

Body

1. First Main Point:

   A. Subpoint:

      1. Sub-subpoint:

      2. Sub-subpoint:

   B. Supporting Point:

      1. Sub-subpoint:

      2. Sub-subpoint:

Transition:

II. Second Main Point:

   A. Subpoint:

      1. Sub-subpoint:

      2. Sub-subpoint:

   B. Subpoint:

      1. Sub-subpoint:

      2. Sub-subpoint:

Transition:

III. Third Main Point:

   A. Subpoint:

      1. Sub-subpoint:

      2. Sub-subpoint:

B. Subpoint:

    1. Sub-subpoint:

    2. Sub-subpoint:

Transition:

Conclusion

I.   Thesis restatement:

II. Main point summary:

III. Clincher:

Name: _____ Section: _____

Title of Speech: _____

INSTRUCTOR CRITIQUE FORM
THE SPEECH OF NARRATION

Rating Scale 7 6 5 4 3 2 1
(Excellent)   (Poor)

Delivery	**Critique**	**Points**

Use of Voice: Intelligibility (rate, volume, pitch, quality, enunciation, pronunciation)? Conversational style? Emotional expression (sincerity)?

Use of Body: Attire? Poise (no distracting cues)? Eye contact?

Structure

Macrostructure: Attention catcher? Listener Relevance? Speaker Credibility? Thesis statement? Preview? Transitions? Thesis restatement? Summary of main points? Clincher?

Microstructure: Language (clear, inclusive)? Technical jargon defined? Slang? Vocalized pauses (verbal garbage—"uh," "um," "like," "ya' know")?

Content

Analysis: Illustrate a moral? Appropriate focus (time constraint)? Personally significant?

Supporting Material: Relevant? Distributed throughout? Personal experiences, definitions, explanations, and examples?

Total Points: _____

Critic (your name): _____ Section: _____

Speaker (person you critiqued): _____

CLASSMATE CRITIQUE FORM
THE SPEECH OF NARRATION

Delivery	**CRITIQUE** (Identify something the speaker did well and why. Identify something the speaker could do to improve, why, and how.)
Use of Voice: Intelligibility (rate, volume, pitch, quality, enunciation, pronunciation)? Conversational style? Emotional expression (sincerity)?	
Use of Body: Attire? Poise (no distracting cues)? Eye contact?	

Structure	**CRITIQUE** (Identify something the speaker did well and why. Identify something the speaker could do to improve, why, and how.)
Macrostructure: Attention catcher? Listener Relevance? Speaker Credibility? Thesis statement? Preview? Transitions? Thesis restatement? Summary of main points? Clincher?	
Microstructure: Language (clear, inclusive)? Technical jargon defined? No Slang? No vocalized pauses?	

Content	**CRITIQUE** (Identify something the speaker did well and why. Identify something the speaker could do to improve, why, and how.)
Analysis: Illustrate a moral? Appropriate focus (time constraint)? Listener Relevance?	
Supporting Material: Relevant? Distributed throughout? Personally significant? Definitions, Examples? Explanations?	

Name:_____Section:_____

SELF-CRITIQUE FORM:
THE SPEECH OF NARRATION

Goal: To evaluate your own performance.

Rationale: As a form of cognitive restructuring, this exercise can help reduce public speaking anxiety while it helps you improve as a public speaker.

Directions: (a) In groups of 4 to 6 students, discuss your last speech performance based on the following guidelines. Then, complete and turn in this form based on your thoughts and the group discussion. OR **(b)** Watch a videotape of yourself giving your last speech. Complete this form and turn it in.

1. In terms of **Delivery,** the requirements for this speech were to sound intelligible, conversational, and sincere; and to look poised, wear appropriate attire, and use effective eye contact. I did the following things well in my last speech:

a.

b.

2. In terms of **Content,** the requirements were to be within the time constraint, illustrate a moral, and use personal experiences, definitions, explanations, and examples. I did the following things well in my last speech:

a.

b.

3. In terms of **Structure,** the requirements were to offer all macrostructural elements, use clear and inclusive language, no slang, and no verbal garbage. I did the following things well in my last speech:

a.

b.

4. If I could do my last speech over again, I would do the following things differently:

a.

b.

c.

5. Overall, I would give myself a grade of _____ on my last speech because . . .

6. To improve as a public speaker on my next speech, I am going to try to:

a.

b.

THE SPEECH OF INFORMATION AND DIVERSITY

Description: This is a 4- to 6-minute informative speech that uses at least two presentational aids, or one that is used in three *different* ways. You must take a multicultural perspective in the specific purpose of this speech. You may elect to compare and/or contrast an aspect of two cultural groups OR you may elect to discuss an aspect of one cultural group in detail. You must, however, step outside your own cultural perspective in some way. Listener relevance must be included for each main point of the speech. The lectern is not allowed for this speech. An extemporaneous delivery style (using a key word outline) is required. Points will be deducted for going over or under the time limits, for not using a *speaking outline* on your notecards, or for using more than five 3 x 5 inch notecards (one side only).

Rationale: There are two primary reasons for requiring this speech. First, thanks to the technology explosion and the information age, we live in an age of diversity. In other words, no one can expect to live their life without encountering people who hold different values, beliefs, and attitudes. Conducting research about the similarities and differences between cultural groups may help students come to respect diversity as a fact of life. Second, most speeches conducted beyond the classroom walls DO employ presentational aids. Aids help ensure that diverse learning styles are addressed. This speech provides an opportunity to construct and integrate effective presentational aids.

Possible Brainstorming Approach:

(1) After brainstorming, select a cultural group that interests you:

(2) Consider an *event* or an *object* or a *custom* or a *belief* or an *issue* that seems unique to that group:

(3) Select one item from #2 for your speech:

(4) Research the item:

(5) Prepare a speech by comparing/contrasting the item as it represents the cultural group you have selected to an event, object, custom, or belief held by the dominant American culture:

OR

(6) Prepare a speech by comparing/contrasting the item as it represents the cultural group you have selected to an event, object, custom, or belief held by another cultural group.

THE SPEECH OF INFORMATION AND DIVERSITY
GRADING CRITERIA

Delivery

Use of Voice:

- Intelligible, conversational, and sincere.
- Fluency. Your ideas should be articulated *fluently*, (achieved through oral rehearsal in advance).
- Emotional Expression. You should sound enthusiastic about sharing this information with us. If you sound bored with your speech, your listeners will not be interested in it either. Vary your rate, pitch, and volume to reinforce the emotion or attitude conveyed in the verbal message.

Use of Body:

- Attire, poise, and eye contact.
- Facial expression. Your facial expressions should reinforce the attitude or emotional stance you are conveying in the verbal message. You should look like you are enthusiastic about sharing this information with us. Practice by looking into a mirror as you rehearse.
- Gestures. Use gestures that reinforce important points or clarify structure. Extend gracefully from the elbow. Do you *appear* to use gestures naturally?
- Motivated movement. Although this is not "required," it is an added PLUS if you can do so in ways that clarify structure or emphasize important points, and gracefully remain "open" to your audience.

Structure

Macrostructure:

- All elements must be clearly articulated.
- Creativity. Attempt to be creative/novel as you develop your attention catcher, listener relevance speaker credibility, thesis statement, transitions, and clincher. Apathy among listeners can be high when speaking to inform. Novelty and creativity can reduce apathy.

Microstructure:

- Inclusive, concrete, jargon defined, no slang, very few vocalized pauses.
- Language. Use colorful descriptors to increase listener involvement (connotative meanings, adjectives, adverbs, sensory language, and figures of speech that add novelty and make it more "fun" to listen). Also use language that demonstrates respect for the diverse perspective you are describing.
- Style. Use internal summaries and connectives (for example, to clarify, moreover, etc.), parallel phrasing, clever turns with phrases, and so forth to create a more fluent style and more novelty (to increase listener retention).

Content

Analysis/Reasoning:

- Be descriptive and within the time constraint.
- Listener relevance must be addressed for each main point.
- You must share "new" knowledge or insight, beyond what your audience is likely to know.
- You must, in some way, step outside your own cultural belief system.
- You must address each learning style somewhere in your speech.

Supporting Materials:

- You must cite at least four oral footnotes from different types of sources during the speech. These sources must be varied, distributed throughout the speech, and properly credited.
- Evidence. You must use different kinds of supporting material as evidence throughout your speech (examples, analogies, testimonies, surveys, facts, statistics, etc.).

Presentational Aids:

- You must use two presentational aids (or one used in at least three DIFFERENT ways).
- Construction. Your aid must offer information a different symbol system that is NOT VER-BAL (You can use pictures, diagrams, charts, graphs, etc.). It must enhance what is offered in the verbal message. Is it large, neat, colorful, and clear? If you take the visual from a source, you must cite that source orally and/or on the visual aid.
- Integration. Do you use it smoothly during the presentation? Do you conceal and disclose it appropriately? Do you reference it effectively with gestures during the speech?

INFORMATION AND DIVERSITY
SPEECH OUTLINE EXAMPLE

Formal Outline: "Japanese Clothing"

Shannon Scott

Introduction

I. **Attention Catcher:** Many of you have worn or seen them.

II. **Listener Relevance:** We can learn a great deal about a culture by examining their clothing.

III. **Speaker Credibility:** I have studied Japanese Martial Arts.

IV. **Thesis:** Today, let's examine the cultural implications of historical Japanese clothing.

V. **Preview of Main Points:** We'll discuss why these outfits evolved as they did, what they meant to the people who wore them, and how these outfits actually show an aspect of Japanese culture: honor.

Body

I. **First Main Point:** Outfits like this evolved out of necessity. (VISUAL AID)

Listener Relevance: Clothing in Japan is no different than clothing of any culture. Clothing serves a purpose of necessity much in the same way as when we dress in heavy coats in the winter.

A. **Subpoint:** War over the territories in Japan was fairly constant.

B. **Subpoint:** No one could know when a fight would break out, so it was impossible for most to rely on armor—which is why it is so rare and valuable today. *(New York Times, January 16,1992)*

C. **Subpoint:** People also had to contend with water, making metal more of a disadvantage than an advantage.

Transition: While these outfits started out as simple necessity, they began to carry cultural meaning.

II. **Second Main Point:** Clothing began to carry meaning.

Listener Relevance: Clothing has always carried some form of meaning. Whether it was peace signs of the seventies or today's "grunge," people choose clothing because of a meaning it portrays.

A. **Subpoint:** Most people wore simple GI's like this one.

B. **Subpoint:** Those who didn't have to work or fight wore silk robes-kosode. These began to symbolize prosperity. **(*New York Times*, January 24, 1993)**

C. **Subpoint:** Some took this fashion statement to the extreme, wearing robes made of five triple layers of silk. Weighing in at 66 pounds, these junihitoe actually contributed to the low life expectancy of women in Japan. **(*Parabola*, Fall, 1994)**

Transition: Along with telling us about the specific people who wore them, these outfits can also tell us a lot about the culture as a whole.

III. **Third Main Point:** Honor played a role in clothing.

    Listener Relevance: Clothing in the United States Armed Forces also carries meaning. Think about the stripes and badges you have seen on the coats of various soldiers.

    A. **Subpoint:** The way a person wears their clothing indicates their status as a combatant.

        1. **Sub-subpoint:** Combatants wore their robes with the left lapel on the outside. This allowed freedom of movement with a weapon strung on the left side of the body. Most carried weapons this way to fight right-handed, keeping their heart farthest from the opponent.

        2. **Sub-subpoint:** The non-combatants folded their outer robes with the right lapel over the left. These included children, elderly, infirm, and women. Also, a warrior was always buried as a non-combatant.

        3. **Sub-subpoint:** It violated honor codes to kill a non-combatant.

    B. **Subpoint:** This method of dress is still evident (though far less life-threatening) in the clothing we wear today.

    C. **Subpoint:** The first Empress of Japan changed much of this when she assumed the throne in 1868. Haruko began to wear Western dresses, without lapels to avoid this statement of non-combatancy. ***(The Historian, Summer, 1993)***

Conclusion

I. **Thesis restatement:** Hopefully, this has helped you gain a better understanding of the implications of another culture's clothing.

II. **Main point summary:** Today we've discussed the evolution of Japanese clothing, the meaning that many took from their wardrobes, and what this tells us about Japanese cultural ideas about honor.

III. **Clincher:** So the next time you wear one or see one, you will know what it really means to the Japanese.

References

Draper, Ellen Dooling. Junihitoe: Silk and suffering. *Parabola*, Fall 1994, 88-90.

Hastings, Sally A. The empress' new clothes and Japanese women. *The Historian*, Summer 1993, 677-695.

Reif, Rita. In old Japan, silk robes were wrapped in beauty. *New York Times*, January 24, 1993, H3 1.

Reif, Rita. Still fierce, but now fashionable. *New York Times*, January 16, 1992, C2.

INFORMATION AND DIVERSITY
SPEECH OUTLINE EXAMPLE

Formal Outline: "Is That Kosher?"

Katherine Harrison

Introduction

I. **Attention Catcher:** You're in your car, dropping a friend off at her house. You slow down just before you get to her house and ask, "Is it Kosher if I pull into the driveway?" Kosher. What does that word mean? Actually it's a Yiddish word meaning fit or proper, and to an observant Jewish person, it means fit to eat.

II. **Speaker Credibility:** I am observant of many Jewish laws, including some Kosher rules. I have cooked in a Kosher kitchen and have eaten countless Kosher meals.

III. **Listener Relevance:** Link: This explanation of Kosher will clarify why some Jewish people don't eat pork and explain what you might find in a Kosher Deli.

IV. **Thesis Statement:** The Kosher diet involves many rules that instruct Jews about what foods are appropriate to eat. This tradition shapes the lives of many Jews around the world, serving as a daily reminder of culture and belief.

V. **Preview:** First I will explain the significance of Kosher, then I will describe what foods qualify as Kosher and, finally, I will talk about how they are prepared.

Body

I. **First Main Point:** Why Kosher?

  A. **Subpoint:** Kosher is actually rooted in Biblical origin, that is, a mitzvah.

    1. **Sub-subpoint:** Health reason for Kosher is a myth. Kosher is a commandment (Gordis, 1995, p. 110).

    2. **Sub-subpoint:** Kosher makes the ordinary extraordinary.

    3. **Sub-subpoint:** Kosher is a reminder of one's devotion to God.

  B. **Subpoint:** Kosher solidifies a community.

    1. **Sub-subpoint:** Kosher helps make Judaism a regular part of daily life (Gordis, 1995, p. 112).

    2. **Sub-subpoint:** Kosher determines a child's connection to Judaism as an adult.

    3. **Sub-subpoint:** Kosher is similar to other communities and their traditions, for example, Norwegians and Lutefisk (Gowin, 2001). **(Listener Relevance)**

Transition: In comparison to other communities and their traditions, the tradition of Kosher is equally significant to the Jewish community. Now let's look at the details of the tradition, including the pork explanation.

II. **Second Main Point:** What is Kosher?

   A. **Subpoint:** *Kosher* means something is fit to eat, compared to *treif*, which means unfit to eat.

   B. **Subpoint:** Let's talk about what Kosher meat consists of (Hofman, 1997, p. 4).

     1. **Sub-subpoint:** Kosher animals have split hooves and chew cud.

     2. **Sub-subpoint:** Cows, goats, and most poultry is Kosher.

     3. **Sub-subpoint:** Pigs, rabbits, birds of prey are not Kosher because they don't have split hooves and chew cud.

   C. **Subpoint:** Let's talk about Kosher dairy products (Hofman, 1997, p. 4).

     1. **Sub-subpoint:** Any milk from a Kosher animal is Kosher.

     2. **Sub-subpoint:** Milk cannot be mixed with meat.

   D. **Subpoint:** Kosher parve is also okay (Hofman, 1997, p. 4).

     1. **Sub-subpoint:** Fruits and vegetables are examples.

     2. **Sub-subpoint:** Eggs are another example.

     3. **Sub-subpoint:** Fish scales and fins are also examples.

       a. **Sub-sub-subpoint:** This means salmon, whitefish, halibut, herring, and bass are Kosher.

       b. **Sub-sub-subpoint:** This also means shellfish (shrimp, crab, lobster) and bottom feeders (catfish) are not Kosher.

Transition: Being Kosher is not just an excuse to turn down oysters at a restaurant. There are also rules about the preparation of Kosher food that are practiced at the butcher and grocer, in the home, and even at Kosher delis.

III. **Third Main Point:** How are foods prepared?

   A. **Subpoint:** Meat slaughtering must adhere to certain rules (Hofman, 1997, p. 4)

     1. **Sub-subpoint:** Meat must be cut across the jugular, and with a sharpened knife.

     2. **Sub-subpoint:** Remove all blood by salting.

   B. **Subpoint:** Meat and milk adheres to certain rules.

     1. **Sub-subpoint:** One cannot mix milk and meat in preparing, serving, washing, or storing.

       a. **Sub-sub-subpoint:** "You shall not boil a kid in its mothers milk." (Exodus 23:19, Holy Bible).

       b. **Sub-sub-subpoint:** This reference is made three times in the Holy Bible.

     2. **Sub-subpoint:** In a Kosher deli you'll find no turkey and Swiss, and you'll find no cheeseburger. But you won't want to forget the pickle with your corned beef on rye. **(Listener Relevance)**

     3. **Sub-subpoint:** You'll also use two sets of dishes and utensils, stored separately.

4. **Sub-subpoint:** There are varying levels of observance of Kosher, which is similar to recycling (**Listener Relevance**).

Transition: This brief explanation of the laws of Kashrut is not complete, but it does give you an idea of how Kosher has served to maintain the distinct, thriving Jewish community in presence of other religious and ethnic diversity.

Conclusion

I. **Thesis restatement:** Observation of Jewish law such as Kosher enables Jews to connect to their religious community and themselves.

II. **Main point summary:** I hope I may have enlightened everyone on a different cultural perspective by explaining why Kosher is a significant Jewish custom, what Kosher means, and how Kosher foods are prepared and served.

III. **Clincher:** So the next time someone asks you, "Is that Kosher?"—you'll know!

References

Gordis, D. (1995). *God was not in the fire.* Touchstone: New York.

Gowin, J. (29 Jan. 2001). Personal Interview.

Hofman, Ethel G. (1997). *Everyday cooking for the Jewish home.* Harper Collins: New York.

Tanakh: A new translation of the Hebrew scriptures according to the traditional Hebrew text. (1985). Jewish Publication Society: Philadelphia.

Name _____ Section _____

Title of Speech _____

PREPARATION OUTLINE
THE SPEECH OF INFORMATION AND DIVERSITY

Introduction

I.   Attention Catcher:

II. Listener Relevance Link:

III. Speaker Credibility:

IV. Thesis Statement:

V.   Preview of Speech:

Body

I.   First Main Point:

    A. Subpoint:

        1. Sub-subpoint:

        2. Sub-subpoint:

    B. Supporting Point:

        1. Sub-subpoint:

        2. Sub-subpoint:

Transition:

II. Second Main Point:

    A. Subpoint:

        1. Sub-subpoint:

        2. Sub-subpoint:

    B. Subpoint:

        1. Sub-subpoint:

        2. Sub-subpoint:

Transition:

III. Third Main Point:

    A. Subpoint:

        1. Sub-subpoint:

        2. Sub-subpoint:

      B. Subpoint:

         1. Sub-subpoint:

         2. Sub-subpoint:

Transition:

Conclusion

I.   Restatement of Thesis:

II. Summary of Main Points:

III. Clincher:

References

List the references you used in the speech. Format them according to APA style (see Chapter 7 in your text for examples).

Name: _____ Section: _____

Title of Speech: _____

INSTRUCTOR CRITIQUE FORM
THE SPEECH OF INFORMATION AND DIVERSITY

Rating Scale   7   6   5   4   3   2   1
            (Excellent)   (Poor)

Delivery	Critique	Points
Use of Voice: Intelligibility (rate, volume, pitch, quality, enunciation, pronunciation)? Conversational style? Fluency? Emotional expression (vocal variety, enthusiasm)?		
Use of Body: Attire? Poise (no distracting cues)? Eye contact? Facial expression? Gestures?		
Structure		
Macrostructure: Attention catcher? Listener Relevance? Speaker Credibility? Thesis statement? Preview? Transitions? Thesis restatement? Summary of main points? Clincher? Creativity?		
Microstructure: Language (clear, accuate, vivid, inclusive, colorful)? Technical jargon defined? Slang? Vocalized pauses (verbal garbage— "uh," "um," "like," "ya' know")? Connectives? Internal summaries?		
Content		
Analysis: Supporting points (accurate, varied depth, related to thesis)? "New" knowledge or insight? Appropriate focus? Listener Relevance? Learning Styles?		
Supporting Material: Relevant? Recent? Varied? Credible? Clear? Distributed throughout? Properly credited? At least four?		
Presentation Aid:		
Construction (large, neat, colorful, Clear, symbol system)? Integration (concealed/disclosed, referenced, smoothly demonstrated)?		

Total Points: _____

Critic (your name): _____ Section: _____

Speaker (person you critiqued): _____

CLASSMATE CRITIQUE FORM
THE SPEECH OF INFORMATION AND DIVERSITY

Delivery	**CRITIQUE** (Identify something the speaker did well and why. Identify something the speaker could do to improve, why, and how.)
Use of Voice: Intelligibility (rate, volume, pitch, quality, enunciation, pronunciation)? Conversational style? Fluency? Emotional expression (vocal variety, enthusiasm)?	
Use of Body: Attire? Poise (no distracting cues)? Eye contact? Facial Expression? Gestures?	

Structure

Macrostructure: Attention catcher? Listener Relevance? Speaker Credibility? Thesis statement? Preview? Transitions? Thesis restatement? Summary of main points? Clincher? Creativity?	
Microstructure: Language (clear, accurate, vivid, inclusive, colorful)? Style (novelty, connectives, phrasing)? Technical jargon defined? No Slang? No vocalized pauses	

Content

Analysis: Supporting points (appropriate, thematic, breadth, depth, listener relevance)? "New knowledge or insight? Appropriate focus? Learning Styles?	
Supporting Material: Relevant? Recent? Varied? Credible? Clear? Distributed throughout? Properly credited? At least four?	

Presentation Aid:

Construction (large, neat, colorful, clear, symbol system)? Integration (concealed/disclosed, referenced, smoothly demonstrated)?	

Name:_____Section:_____

SELF-CRITIQUE FORM:
THE SPEECH OF INFORMATION AND DIVERSITY

Goal: To evaluate your own performance.

Rationale: As a form of cognitive restructuring, this exercise can help reduce public speaking anxiety while it helps you improve as a public speaker.

Directions: (a) In groups of 4 to 6 students, discuss your last speech performance based on the following guidelines. Then, complete and turn in this form based on your thoughts and the group discussion. OR **(b)** Watch a videotape of yourself giving your last speech. Complete this form and turn it in.

1. In terms of **Delivery,** the requirements for this speech were to sound intelligible, conversational, and sincere; and to look poised, wear appropriate attire, use effective eye contact, facial expression, and gestures. I did the following things well in my last speech:

a.

b.

2. In terms of **Content,** the requirements were to be within the time constraint, offer new knowledge or insight, round the cycle of learning, and of depth, breadth and listener relevance. I did the following things well in my last speech:

a.

b.

3. In terms of **Structure,** the requirements were to offer all macrostructural elements in a creative way, use clear, inclusive, and colorful language, use no slang or verbal garbage, and use style in connectives and phrasing. I did the following things well in my last speech:

a.

b.

4. In terms of presentational aids, the requirements were to construct and integrate them effectively. I did the following things well in my last speech:

a.

b.

5. If I could do my last speech over again, I would do the following things differently:

a.

b.

c.

6. Overall, I would give myself a grade of _____ on my last speech because . . .

7. To improve as a public speaker on my next speech, I am going to try to:
a.

b.

THE SPEECH OF DEFINITION

Description:
This is a 4- to 6- minute informative speech that uses at least two presentational aids, or one that is used in three different ways. The specific purpose of this speech is to reduce ambiguity by illustrating how one term or concept can be defined in many different ways. Your ultimate goal is to make an abstract concept more concrete for your listeners. The term or concept you select might come from a language other than English. Your supporting material should include both denotative and connotative definitions as well as examples and explanations. Listener relevance must be included for each main point of the speech. The lectern is not allowed for this speech. Points will be deducted for going over or under the time limits, for not using a speaking outline (key words and phrases), or for using more than five 3 x 5 inch index cards (one side only).

Rationale:
There are two primary reasons for requiring this speech. First, thanks to the technology explosion and the information age, we live in an age of diversity. In other words, no one can expect to live their life without encountering people who hold different values, beliefs, and attitudes. As such, many terms and concepts have multiple meanings. This speech is designed to help students realize the need to avoid making assumptions about the meanings of abstract terms and concepts. Second, most speeches conducted beyond the classroom walls DO employ presentational aids. Aids help ensure that diverse learning styles are addressed. This speech provides an opportunity to construct and integrate effectively presentational aids.

GRADING CRITERIA
THE SPEECH OF DEFINITION

Delivery

Use of Voice:

- Intelligible, conversational, and sincere.
- Fluency. Your ideas should be articulated fluently, (achieved through oral rehearsal in advance).
- Emotional Expression. You should sound enthusiastic about sharing this information with us. If you sound bored with your speech, your listeners will not be interested in it either. Vary your rate, pitch, and volume to reinforce the emotion or attitude conveyed in the verbal message.

Use of Body:

- Attire, poise, and eye contact.
- Facial expression. Your facial expressions should reinforce the attitude or emotional stance you are conveying in the verbal message. You should look like you are enthusiastic about sharing this information with us. Practice by looking into a mirror as you rehearse.
- Gestures. Use gestures that reinforce important points or clarify structure. Extend gracefully from the elbow. Do you appear to use gestures naturally?
- Motivated movement. Although this is not "required," it is an added PLUS if you can do so in ways that clarify structure or emphasize important points, and gracefully remain "open" to your audience.

Structure

Macrostructure:

- All elements must be clearly articulated.
- Creativity. Attempt to be creative/novel as you develop your attention catcher, listener relevance speaker credibility, thesis statement, transitions, and clincher. Apathy among listeners can be high when speaking to inform. Novelty and creativity can reduce apathy.

Microstructure:

- Inclusive, concrete, jargon defined, no slang, very few vocalized pauses.
- Language. Use colorful descriptors to increase listener involvement (connotative meanings, adjectives, and adverbs that add novelty and make it more "fun" to listen). Also use language that demonstrates respect for the diverse perspective you are describing.
- Style. Use internal summaries and connectives (for example, to clarify, moreover, etc.), parallel phrasing, clever turns with phrases, and so forth to create a more fluent style and more novelty (to increase listener retention).

Content

Analysis/Reasoning:

- Be descriptive and within the time constraint.
- Listener relevance must be addressed for each main point.
- You must share "new" knowledge or insight, beyond what your audience is likely to know.
- You must round the cycle of learning.

Supporting Materials:

- You must cite at least four oral footnotes from different sources during the speech. These sources must be varied, distributed throughout the speech, and properly credited.
- Evidence. You must use different kinds of supporting material as evidence throughout your speech (examples, analogies, testimonies, surveys, facts, statistics, etc.).

Presentational Aids:

- You must use two presentational aids (or one used in at least three DIFFERENT ways).
- Construction. Your aid must offer information a different symbol system that is NOT VERBAL (You can use pictures, diagrams, charts, graphs, etc.). It must enhance what is offered in the verbal message. Is it large, neat, colorful, and clear? If you take the visual from a source, you must cite that source on the visual aid.
- Integration. Do you use it smoothly during the presentation? Do you conceal and disclose it appropriately? Do you reference it effectively with gestures during the speech?

Name: _____   Section: _____

Title of Speech: _____

PREPARATION OUTLINE
THE SPEECH OF DEFINITION

Introduction

I.   Attention Catcher:

II. Listener Relevance Link:

III. Speaker Credibility:

IV. Thesis Statement:

V.   Preview of Speech:

Body

I.   First Main Point:

   A. Subpoint:

      1. Sub-subpoint:

      2. Sub-subpoint:

   B. Supporting Point:

      1. Sub-subpoint:

      2. Sub-subpoint:

   Transition:

II. Second Main Point:

   A. Subpoint:

      1. Sub-subpoint:

      2. Sub-subpoint:

   B. Subpoint:

      1. Sub-subpoint:

      2. Sub-subpoint:

   Transition:

III. Third Main Point:

   A. Subpoint:

      1. Sub-subpoint:

      2. Sub-subpoint:

    B. Subpoint:

       1. Sub-subpoint:

       2. Sub-subpoint:

Transition:

Conclusion

I.   Restatement of Thesis:

II. Summary of Main Points:

III. Clincher:

References

List the references you used in the speech. Format them according to APA style (see Chapter 7 in your text for examples).

Name: _____ Section: _____

Title of Speech: _____

INSTRUCTOR CRITIQUE FORM
THE SPEECH OF DEFINITION

Rating Scale 7 6 5 4 3 2 1
(Excellent)   (Poor)

Delivery	Critique	Points
Use of Voice: Intelligibility (rate, volume, pitch, quality, enunciation, pronunciation)? Conversational style? Fluency? Emotional expression (vocal variety, enthusiasm)?		
Use of Body: Attire? Poise (no distracting cues)? Eye contact? Facial expression? Gestures?		
Structure		
Macrostructure: Attention catcher? Listener Relevance? Speaker Credibility? Thesis statement? Preview? Transitions? Thesis restatement? Summary of main points? Clincher? Creativity?		
Microstructure: Language (clear, accuate, vivid, inclusive, colorful)? Technical jargon defined? Slang? Vocalized pauses (verbal garbage— "uh," "um," "like," "ya' know")? Connectives? Internal summaries?		
Content		
Analysis: Supporting points (accurate, varied depth, related to thesis)? "New knowledge or insight? Appropriate focus? Listener Relevance? Learning Styles?		
Supporting Material: Relevant? Recent? Varied? Credible? Clear? Distributed throughout? Properly credited? At least four?		
Presentational Aids:		
Construction (large, neat, colorful, Clear, symbol system)? Integration (concealed/disclosed, referenced, smoothly demonstrated)?		

Total Points: _____

Critic (your name): _____ Section: _____

Speaker (person you critiqued): _____

CLASSMATE CRITIQUE FORM
THE SPEECH OF DEFINITION

Delivery	**CRITIQUE (Identify something the speaker did well and why. Identify something the speaker could do to improve, why, and how.)**
Use of Voice: Intelligibility (rate,volume, pitch, quality, enunciation, pronunciation)? Conversational style? Emotional expression (vocal variety, sincerity)?	
Use of Body: Attire? Poise (no distracting cues)? Eye contact?Facial Expression? Gestures?	

Structure	**CRITIQUE (Identify something the speaker did well and why. Identify something the speaker could do to improve, why, and how.)**
Macrostructure: Attention catcher? Listener Relevance? Speaker Credibility? Thesis statement? Preview? Transitions? Thesis restatement? Summary of main points? Clincher? Creativity?	
Microstructure: Language (clear, accurate, vivid, inclusive, colorful)? Style (novelty, connectives, phrasing)? Technical jargon defined? No Slang? No vocalized pauses?	

Content	**CRITIQUE (Identify something the speaker did well and why. Identify something the speaker could do to improve, why, and how.)**
Analysis: Supporting points (accurate, varied, depth, related to thesis)? "New" knowledge or insight? Appropriate focus? Listener Relevance? Learning styles? Appropriate focus (time constraint)? Listener Relevance?	
Supporting Material: Relevant? Recent? Varied? Credible? Clear? Distributed throughout? Properly credited? At least four?	

Presentational Aid	**CRITIQUE (Identify something the speaker did well and why. Identify something the speaker could do to improve, why, and how.)**
Construction (large, neat, colorful, clear, symbol system)? Integration (concealed/ disclosed, referenced, smoothly demonstrated?	

Name:_____ Section:_____

SELF-CRITIQUE FORM:
THE SPEECH OF DEFINITION

Goal: To evaluate your own performance.

Rationale: As a form of cognitive restructuring, this exercise can help reduce public speaking anxiety while it helps you improve as a public speaker.

Directions: (a) In groups of 4 to 6 students, discuss your last speech performance based on the following guidelines. Then, complete and turn in this form based on your thoughts and the group discussion. OR **(b)** Watch a videotape of yourself giving your last speech. Complete this form and turn it in.

1. In terms of **Delivery,** the requirements for this speech were to sound intelligible, conversational, and sincere; and to look poised, wear appropriate attire, use effective eye contact, facial expression, and gestures. I did the following things well in my last speech:

   a.

   b.

2. In terms of **Content,** the requirements were to be within the time constraint, offer new knowledge or insight as well as listener relevance, round the cycle of learning, and offer depth, breadth and listener relevance. I did the following things well in my last speech:

   a.

   b.

3. In terms of **Structure,** the requirements were to offer all macrostructural elements in a creative way, use clear, inclusive, and colorful language, use no slang or verbal garbage, and use style in connectives and phrasing. I did the following things well in my last speech:

   a.

   b.

4. In terms of presentational aids, the requirements were to construct and integrate them effectively. I did the following things well in my last speech:

   a.

   b.

5. If I could do my last speech over again, I would do the following things differently:

a.

b.

c.

6. Overall, I would give myself a grade of _____ on my last speech because . . .

7. To improve as a public speaker on my next speech, I am going to try to:

a.

b.

PERSUAVIVE SPEECHES

Speeches to persuade attempt to change listeners in some way. Dispositional persuasive speeches attempt to change listeners' beliefs, values, or attitudes about something. Actuation persuasive speeches, on the other hand, go a step beyond dispositional speeches to also attempt to change the behavior of listeners and/or some faction of society. For example, if I tried to convince you that recycling is a good thing to do, that is a dispositional persuasive speech. If I also try to get you to change your recycling habits, then I am engaged in an actuation persuasive speech. Dispositional persuasive speeches tend to focus on claims of fact or questions of value, whereas actuation persuasive speeches tend to focus on claims of policy.

Thesis statements that arise from *claims of fact* are focused on something people believe may or may not be true. Debate exists as to whether or not the fact is, indeed, a fact. The question may be about whether something actually happened or not (i.e., evolution versus creation). The question might be about whether something does or does not exist (there is/is not intelligent life on other planets). The question might be causal (smoking causes/does not cause cancer). Or the question of fact might come in the form of a prediction (the Minnesota Vikings will/will not win the SuperBowl next year). Claims of fact, then, are thesis statement focused on debatable issues that attempt to convince listeners that something:

■ did or did not exist (or occur)

■ does or does not exist (or occur)

■ does or does not cause

■ will or will not occur

Claims of value also help shape a thesis statement for a dispositional persuasive speech. Claims of value focus on a debatable belief about what is good/bad, moral/immoral, "right"/"wrong," just/unjust, and so forth. Some examples of dispositional persuasive speeches focused on claims of value include:

■ George W. Bush deserves (does not deserve) to be rated as an effective President.

■ Euthanasia is moral (immoral).

■ Capital punishment is fair (unfair).

■ Spanking children is right (wrong).

Claims of policy shape a thesis statement for an actuation persuasive speech. They attempt to change behavior by calling listeners to action to solve a problem. The thesis statement is usually phrased in a way that uses the words "should" or "should not." It always implies action of some kind. Some examples of actuation persuasive speeches focused on claims of policy include:

- The United States government should (should not) raise taxes.
- The city of Fargo should (should not) develop a better flood control system.
- The state legislature should (should not) increase funding for higher education.
- The university should (should not) build a pedestrian bridge between the parking lot and campus.
- People should (should not) be fined for not calling for help when they witness a crime.

DETERMINING YOUR TARGET AUDIENCE

For any persuasive speech you present, all members of your audience may not share the same opinion. In other words, some of your audience members may already agree with you, some may be opposed to your position, and some may be undecided. The degree to which you may attempt to persuade listeners is based on the mix of beliefs represented in your audience. If most of your listeners are opposed to your claim, you might limit how far you hope to persuade them. For example, if you were to present a pro-choice speech to a group of people representing the Catholic diocese, you could safely assume that most of your listeners are opposed to your position. You might be more successful if you limit the degree to which you are persuading. You might try to convince them that abortion is OK when the alternative is certain death for mother and child during delivery. Likewise, if most of your listeners already agree with you, you may want increase the degree to which you want to persuade, moving from an attitudinal to an actuation speech. For example, if you are doing a persuasive speech on recycling and most of your listeners agree that it is a "good" thing (claim of value), you might try to persuade them to recycle more effectively by sorting their plastics, etc. (claim of policy). You can discover the stance of your listeners and your target audience through audience analysis (educated guesses) or by surveying the group.

In any group, your listeners may have mixed beliefs about your topic. You may be helping some listeners form an opinion, attempt to reform the opinions of others, and simply reinforcing the opinions held by others.

- Form: Some listeners may be undecided about the issue you are discussing.
- Reform: Some listeners may be opposed to the issue you are advocating.
- Reinforce: Some listeners may already agree with you about the issue at hand.

Your target audience is the majority belief held by your listeners. This does not mean you ignore the others. All can benefit from your message. It simply helps you determine the *degree to which you might be able to successfully persuade* the group.

THE POINT–COUNTERPOINT SPEECH

Description: This is a 4- to 6-minute dispositional persuasive speech. In other words, you must attempt to form, reform, or reinforce listeners' attitudes or beliefs about an issue. It may focus on a claim of fact or a claim of value. You and a partner will research and prepare two different speeches advocating opposite sides of the same issue. Although you will research and prepare your speeches together using the same type of question (fact or value) to ensure a "clash," you will each be graded individually for you oral presentations. Lectern and presentational aids are optional for this speech. Points will be deducted for going over or under the time limits, for not using a *speaking outline* (key words and phrases), or for using more than five 3 × 5 inch notecards (one side only).

Rationale: This assignment is prepared in dyads to help students begin to realize that there are two defendable sides to any argument. By researching together, students will begin to understand that the same resource can sometimes be used to support either side of an issue. Limiting the assignment to claims of fact and value allows students to experience preparing, presenting, and critiquing dispositional persuasive speeches.

THE SPEECH OF POINT–COUNTERPOINT
ORGANIZATIONAL FORMATS

You will use one of four organizational formats for this speech. Both speakers must use the same organizational format to ensure a direct clash. These formats are the refutative comparative advantages, invitational, and problem (no solution) patterns.

The refutative pattern is topical in nature. In other words, for each main point speakers determine opposing claims. For a speech about whether or not Bigfoot exists, for example, one speaker might claim for the first main point that Bigfoot has been sited by many different people. The other speaker might claim for the first main point that the credentials of those who have cited Bigfoot are questionable. For the second main point, one speaker might contend that Bigfoot has been sighted numerous times over the years. The other speaker might claim for the second main point that the numerous sightings are in too many locations to "make sense." The refutative pattern asks speakers to consider opposing views for each claim/contention/main point addressed.

The comparative advantages pattern asks speakers to develop claims for each main point that argue how the advantages of their approach outweigh the disadvantages posed by the other person. Within each main point, each speaker also argues that the disadvantages of the position advocated by the partner outweigh the advantages. In a speech about the morality of spanking children, one speaker might advocate that spanking teaches children the boundaries for their actions. This outweighs the disadvantages of advocating violence as appropriate since young children do not have the verbal skills to reason effectively. The other speaker might claim that spanking is wrong because it teaches children that hitting is OK. They might cite examples where children play out these behaviors on each other. The speaker would claim that the advantages of using alternative forms of discipline outweigh the disadvantages of taking longer to reason through why certain behavior is appropriate or inappropriate. The comparative advantages pattern asks speakers to develop reasons as to why the advantages of their claim outweigh the disadvantages.

The invitational pattern uses a three-step approach to arranging your main points. In the first main point, offer your perspective and how it works for you. In the second main point, create an atmosphere that encourages mutual understanding. And, in the third main point, focus on positive aspects of a situation and persistence of them.

The problem (no solution) pattern typically uses breadth, depth, and significance of a problem as its main points. Doing so clarifies the "fact" that it is a problem warranting attention.

THE SPEECH OF POINT–COUNTERPOINT
GRADING CRITERIA

Delivery

Use of Voice:

- Intelligible, conversational, and sincere.
- Fluency.
- Emotional Expression. You should sound committed to your opinions about the issue. You need to have *emotional conviction* in your voice or you will never convince your audience to share your opinion.

Use of Body:

- Attire, poise, and eye contact.
- Facial expression, gestures, and motivated movement.
- Initial and terminal ethos (conveyed with pauses and eye contact at the beginning and end of speech).

Structure

Macrostructure:

- All elements must be clearly articulated.
- Creativity. Use organizational format that lends itself to persuasion (refutative comparative advantages, invitational, or problem (no solution)).
- There must be a "clash" between speakers (in organizational design).

Microstructure:

- Inclusive, concrete, jargon defined, no slang, very few vocalized pauses.
- Language. Use persuasive "punch" words in structural comments to enhance pathos.
- Style and use of phrasing that enhances pathos.

Content

Analysis/Reasoning:

- Be descriptive and within the time constraint.
- Listener relevance must be addressed for each main point.
- Each learning style must be addressed.
- Ethos, pathos, and logos must be evident.
- There must be a "clash" between the speakers (in analysis).

Supporting Materials:

- You must cite at least four oral footnotes from different sources during the speech. These sources must be varied, credible to your topic, distributed throughout the speech, and properly credited.
- Evidence. You must use different kinds of supporting material as evidence throughout your speech (examples, analogies, testimonies, surveys, facts, statistics, etc.).

POINT–COUNTERPOINT DISPOSITIONAL PERSUASIVE SPEECH EXAMPLE

Formal Outline: "Pro Greek Life"

Kathy McGrath

Introduction

I. **Attention Catcher:** What do NDSU, academic clubs, college athletics, student government and Greek organizations have in common?

II. **Listener Relevance:** Most of you have seen Greek houses on our campus and may have wondered what they are all about.

III. **Speaker Credibility:** Having been a member of Greek organization, I have experienced the positive aspects of Greek membership.

IV. **Thesis Statement:** Today, I'd like to share some of the benefits of Greek membership with you.

V. **Preview:** Specifically, we will discuss the low cost, positive contributions to personal growth, and benefits of meeting the standards of Greek organizations.

   Transition: So, what did all those groups have in common? They all have criteria set up for choosing their members.

Body

I. **First Main Point:** Like any organization, fraternities and sororities have criteria set up for choosing their members.

   Listener Relevance: These criteria demonstrate the quality standards we all aspire to attain.

   A. **Subpoint:** Grades are an important issue.

      1. **Sub-Subpoint:** NDSU requires a 2.0 (NDSU).

      2. **Sub-Subpoint:** Greek organizations require a 2.0 (Morgan).

   B. **Subpoint:** Greeks choose members through conversations with rushees.

   C. **Subpoint:** Greeks recruit members who can fulfill organizational standards

      1. **Sub-Subpoint:** Sigma Chi Jordan Standard (Jordan Standard 11).

   Transition: Some people think that the cost of membership also makes Greek organizations selective.

II. **Second Main Point:** Greek membership is affordable.

   Listener Relevance: College students living on tight budgets can actually save money by joining a Greek organization.

   A. **Subpoint:** Living in Greek houses is less expensive than living in the dorms.

      1. **Sub-Subpoint:** Heather Schimke's story about moving into Alpha Gamma Delta.

      2. **Sub-Subpoint:** Dorm expenses are $200 a month higher than living in a Greek house (NDSU Graduate Bulletin 196).

B. **Subpoint:** For members living out of house, cost is only about $10 a week (Morgan).

   1. **Sub-Subpoint:** This pays for 3 meals and one social activity every week (Conn).

Transition: Now that you see that Greek living is actually less expensive than living on campus, let's talk about how Greek life enhances your personal development.

III. **Third Main Point:** Greek membership develops positive social skills, strong academic standing, and leadership skills.

   Listener Relevance: These skills will help us achieve our potential personally and professionally.

A. **Subpoint:** According to University statistics, Greek men have a higher GPA than non-Greek men at NDSU. And, Greek women outscore the Greek men by .10 (Morgan).

B. **Subpoint:** Greek membership leads to more opportunities after college.

   1. **Sub-Subpoint:** According to statistics in the 1996 Fraternity rush handbook, 85% of all Fortune 500 companies are headed by Greeks, 76% of our nation's senators are Greek, 43 of the nation's 50 largest corporations are led by Greeks, and all but two Presidents have been Greek since 1825.

C. **Subpoint:** Last, Greek membership promotes positive personal development through programs that increase awareness.

Transition: With all these programs, it is no wonder that Greeks are the most visible groups on campus.

Conclusion

I. **Thesis restatement:** Obviously, there are many positive aspects to Greek membership.

II. **Main point summary:** Clearly because of the low cost, positive programs presented, and standards set by Greek organizations, you can see that Greek membership is a positive addition to any person's college experience.

III. **Clincher:** So, before you decide to dismiss Greek membership, remember all the opportunities you dismiss with it.

References

Conn, C. (1997, March 18). Personal interview.

Morgan, A.M. (1997, March 18). Personal interview.

North Dakota State University fraternity rush handbook. (Fall 1996).

North Dakota State University graduate bulletin. (1996–1998).

Norman Shield: A lifelong commitment to Sigma Chi (34th ed.). (1993).

Schimke, Heather. (1997, March 18). Personal interview.

POINT–COUNTERPOINT DISPOSITIONAL PERSUASIVE SPEECH EXAMPLE

Formal Outline: "The Harm of Greek Letter Organizations"

Kris Treinen

Introduction

I. **Attention Catcher:** James Callahan, a freshman at Rutgers University, died after chugging Kamikazes—"a nerve-numbing mixture of vodka, triple sec and lime juice." An intoxicated, 20-year-old York College student fell off the roof of an apartment building and died (*Time*, April 16, 1990). What do these two stories have in common? Both of them happened as a result of a fraternity party.

II. **Listener Relevance:** Many of you have heard about fraternities and sororities and some of you may have attended a "social function" sponsored by an North Dakota State University Greek Organization.

III. **Speaker Credibility:** Through my research, I have learned about Greek life and Greek organizations.

IV. **Thesis Statement:** Today, I'm here to prove to you that Greek organizations have a harmful effect on NDSU students and students across the nation.

V. **Preview:** Specifically, I will show you why Greek organizations are not economically feasible for all students, how Greek organizations are elitist, and why Greek organizations are not conducive to a student's personal development.

Body

I. **First Main Point:** Greek organizations are not economically feasible for all students.

   Listener Relevance: Many college students living on tight budgets simply cannot afford to join one.

   A. **Subpoint:** According to Ann Marie Morgan, the Assistant Director of Greek Life at NDSU, all students must pay $20.00 to go through sorority formal rush.

   B. **Subpoint:** There is also a one-time new member fee which averages $175 to join an NDSU fraternity.

   C. **Subpoint:** According to the *North Dakota State University Fraternity Life Handbook*, rent and dues for a fraternity average $1200 a semester. Members who don't live in the house pay an average of $200 a semester.

   Transition: The high costs of membership in sororities and fraternities contributes to the Greek system's rituals of exclusion.

II. **Second Main Point:** Greek organizations are elitist.

   Listener Relevance: This elitism can be considered prejudiced and un-American.

A. **Subpoint:** According to George Kuh, Ernest Pascarella and Henry Wechsler in the April 19, 1996 issue of the *Chronicle of Higher Education*, "In terms of race, ethnicity and sexual orientation, fraternities tend to be more homogeneous than the student body in general" (p. 68A).

B. **Subpoint:** An article in the July 4, 1987 issue of *The Nation* quotes a University of Michigan student as saying, "The clubs are 'racist and anti-Semitic by way of pure deletion.' It's not so much as 'us' and 'them'; they're not even articulated as another. If they don't rush your sorority, they simply don't exist" (p. 10).

Transition: Besides being elitist, fraternities and sororities do not provide a healthy environment for students.

III. **Third Main Point:** Greek organizations are not conducive to a student's personal development.

Listener Relevance: Involvement in these organizations can hurt students' chances to succeed, which is why we came to college.

A. **Subpoint:** The initiation rituals that Fraternities and Sororities condone endanger the safety of pledges. The April 29, 1996 *US News and World Report* states: "at least 65 students have died since 1978 as a result of beatings and stress inflicted during fraternity initiation rituals" (p. 26).

B. **Subpoint:** Alcohol abuse is another problem in fraternities and sororities. A study by the Harvard University School of Public Health of more than 17,000 students at 140 randomly selected 4-year colleges, found 86% of those who live in fraternity houses were binge drinkers compared to 45% of non-members (*The Chronicle of Higher Education*, April 19, 1996, p. 68A).

C. **Subpoint:** Alcohol abuse also leads to even more serious problems. M.G. Lord says a 1987 report documented 50 rapes over a 2–3 year period in fraternities. "Charts of how many beers it took to seduce various sorority women are common in fraternity houses" (p. 11).

Transition: The atmosphere which surrounds sororities and fraternities is a negative force in students' lives.

Conclusion

I. **Thesis restatement:** As I have proven today, Greek organizations have a harmful effect on NDSU students and students across the nation.

II. **Main point summary:** Today, I've shown why Greek organizations are not economically feasible for all students, how Greek organizations are elitist, and why Greek organizations are not conducive to students' personal development.

III. **Clincher:** Before you decide to join an NDSU Greek organization, think about the 20-year-old York college student who fell off the roof of an apartment building during an off-campus fraternity party and died. And don't forget James Callahan, who died his freshman year at Rutgers University after chugging Kamikazes at a fraternity party. Was it really worth their lives?

References

Kuh, G.D., Pascarella, E.T., & Wechsler, H. (1996, April 19). The questionable value of fraternities. *The Chronicle of Higher Education 42*, 68A.

Lord, M.G. (1997, July 4). Frats and sororities: The Greek's rites of exclusion. *The Nation*, 245. 10–13.

Morgan, A.M. (1997, March 17). Personal interview.

North Dakota State University. (1996). *North Dakota State University fraternity life* [Brochure].

Stranglin, D. (1996, April 29). Greek tragedies. *US News & World Report 120*, 26.

Tifft, S. (1990, April 16). Waging war on the greeks: fraternities and sororities are being forced to clean up their acts. *Time, 135* 64–65.

POINT–COUNTERPOINT DISPOSITIONAL PERSUASIVE SPEECH EXAMPLE

Formal Outline: "Home Schooling: Superiority and Success"

Dixie Davis

Introduction

I. **Attention Catcher:** Picture this: Your child comes home from school and upon your seemingly harmless inquiry of his day he bursts into a flood of tears. The causes are there, but what do you do?

II. **Listener Relevance:** We are all familiar with that age-old question, "So what did you learn in school today?" But, how often do we really listen to the answer?

III. **Speaker Credibility:** I have done extensive research on the subject of education and have collaborated several problems into one view: The public system is failing. The solution: Home schooling.

IV. **Thesis Statement:** Today, I'll prove that the advantages of home schooling far outweigh the disadvantages.

V. **Preview:** More specifically, we'll reveal how home schooling avoids the violence in public schools, point out its flexibility and convenience as a learning tool, and demonstrate how it helps build strong family and personal relationships.

Body

I. **First Main Point:** Home schooling isolates children from the violence in our public school systems.

   A. **Subpoint (Listener Relevance):** We can all imagine how terrible it would be to have to enter the school everyday wondering if we would come out alive.

   B. **Subpoint:** Violence in public schools has become more and more of an issue in recent years. School shootings such as Columbine in the spring of 1999 have made families realize that the safety and security of schools are inferior.

   C. **Subpoint:** According to Dori Staehle, author of an article in the June 2000 journal, *Roeper Review*, 99% of families have chosen home schooling after coming to the realization that the school has become equivalent to prison. From mandatory security checks to the elimination of backpacks, many American teens can relate to her generalization.

   Transition: Not only does home schooling help kids avoid the violence of the public system, it also offers a variety of learning strategies not available in regular schools.

II. **Second Main Point:** Home schooling offers families flexibility in teaching and learning unavailable in the public education system.

   A. **Subpoint (Listener Relevance):** We all remember the eight hour days and having to schedule appointments and things around school. In a home-schooled environment, this isn't necessary.

152

B. **Subpoint:** The opposition may claim this flexibility leads to less structure and effectiveness, but in reality, quite the contrary is true. However, in the book *Homeschooling for Excellence*, written by David Colfax, a study relevant to this point was conducted. Based on the results, it's easy to see which style is more effective.

C. **Subpoint:** In his book, *The How and Why of Homeschooling*, Ray Ballman refers to two attorneys who enforce the constitutionality of home schooling with amendments.

D. **Subpoint:** According to 'Homeschooled Children,' an article published in a 1999 issue of *Clinical Pediatrics*, in many states parents must follow specific guidelines in educating their children. These include obtaining a teaching certificate, taking attendance, and reviewing progress with local officials.

Transition: Home schooling not only offers a more flexible, yet structured learning style, it also helps to build stronger family and personal relationships.

III. **Third Main Point:** Family and personal relationships are greatly strengthened by home schooling.

A. **Subpoint (Listener Relevance):** Being in college, we start to better appreciate our family and those who love us. Once we step into our first class of 200 people, we realize the value of one-on-one relationships.

B. **Subpoint:** Critics of home schooling may say that this closeness in the family lessens the socialization of children. Maybe they are missing out on the true experience, as Ian Hunter puts it in his article in the *Alberta Report*. However, they are receiving positive rather than negative socialization.

C. **Subpoint:** In an entry written by Deborah Jones in the *Canadian Medical Association Journal*, a home-schooled family is analyzed. Many home schooling families form support networks and cooperate their learning techniques with one another.

D. **Subpoint:** The main basis for home schooling is specialized instruction.

Transition: These attentive relationships built through home schooling are just one of the many advantages it offers.

Conclusion

I. **Thesis restatement:** The advantages of home schooling certainly outweigh the disadvantages.

II. **Main point summary:** Home schooling avoids the violence of public school systems. It provides a flexible and convenient learning and teaching style. And it helps build stronger family and personal relationships.

III. **Clincher:** So if you find yourself asking your child, "What did you learn in school today?" and get a tearful reply, home schooling might be just what you're looking for!

References

Ballman, R. (1987). *The how and why of home schooling.* Westchester: Good News Publishers.

Colfax, D., & Colfax, M. (1987). *Homeschooling for excellence.* Philco: Mountain House Press.

Hunter, I. (2000). Home-schooling forces us to reconsider whether God should have been expelled from public school. *Alberta Report.* pp. 44.

Jones, D. (1999). Homeschooling right prescription for Vancouver MD. *Canadian Medical Association Journal*, vol. 160 Issue 11, p 1676.

Klugewicz, S. (1999). Homeschooled children: A pediatric perspective. *Clinical Pediatrics*, Vol. 38 Issue 7, p 407.

Staehle, D. (2000). Taking a different path: A mother's reflections on homeschooling. *Roeper Review*, Vol. 22 Issue 4, p 270.

POINT–COUNTERPOINT DISPOSITIONAL PERSUASIVE SPEECH EXAMPLE

Formal Outline: "Who Should Teach the Students?"

Robert Maeyaert

Introduction

I. **Attention Catcher:** We tell our children everyday that they can do whatever they want to do, if they only try. We tell them to do their best at whatever they do so that they can live up to their potential. How our children are educated plays a big role as to what their potential is and what they will do with their lives.

II. **Listener Relevance:** All of us have come from different educational backgrounds, from public to private schools, to religious schools, to even home schools.

III. **Speaker Credibility:** After having been exposed to a positive learning environment myself and having done extensive research on this topic, I feel I can speak accurately about it.

IV. **Thesis Statement:** Simply put, the home schooling environment is not the most effective way for our students to learn.

V. **Preview:** To prove this, let's consider issues related to the parents and teachers, the limitations of the home environment itself, and parental involvement as a link to student success.

Body

I. **First Main Point:** A key issue to home schooling rests with the fact that the parent is also the teacher.

    A. **Subpoint:** Many obvious arguments arise without even putting any amount of thought into this issue.

    B. **Subpoint:** The September 1st, 2000 issue of *Maclean's* stated, for example, that for parents, one of the greatest challenges is educating themselves about how – and what – to teach.

    C. **Subpoint:** Many teachers have completed post-secondary education, and some have gone further than that in order to be able to effectively teach children in the areas that they have studied.

        1. **Sub-Subpoint:** According to Ballman in the book, *The How and Why of Home Schooling*, many parents do not take the time to prepare lesson plans for each and every day.

        2. **Sub-Subpoint:** Parents are not going to be the best authorities to provide students with the opportunity to partake in the learning of higher education.

Transition: We have addressed parents as teachers; however, can the home, in most cases, offer us all the other important tools of school?

II. **Second Main Point:** The home school is not a complete alternative to the public or private school environment.

A. **Subpoint:** A February 2nd, 1996 article in the *U. S. News and World Report* stated that Brian Ray of the National Home Education Research Institute found that 76 percent of home schooling parents surveyed in the states of Washington, Utah, and Nevada wanted to enroll their child at least part time in public or private school courses.

B. **Subpoint:** This study further goes on to claim what I stated previously about parents not wanting to take on tougher classes.

    1. **Sub-Subpoint:** According to Colfax in the book, *Homeschooling for Excellence*, kids will work on their studies for a while, and then find something more interesting to do.

    2. **Sub-Subpoint:** Schools have so many resources to offer students. They have the interests of many diverse teachers, as well as access to different scholastic materials. They also have diverse technology and science laboratories that are there to offer students the tools that they need to succeed.

Transition: So far, we have highlighted two major pitfalls of home schooling, one having to do with why parents cannot be effective teachers and the other with the limitations of the home school environment itself. So let's turn now from these kinds of obstacles to clarify what factors will create student success in our school systems.

III. **Third Main Point:** The biggest factor that will determine whether students are successful has to do with parental involvement. Students do not have to be home schooled for their parents to be involved in their education.

A. **Subpoint:** When we use the term parental involvement, we are not in any way saying that parents should home school their children; rather, they should support them.

    1. **Sub-Subpoint:** The journal article in *The World and I*, June 2000, interviewed Kathleen Lyons, a communication director at the National Education Association. Lyons contends, "It takes more than a good heart to be a good teacher."

    2. **Sub-Subpoint:** She went on to conclude that the "common denominator" in student achievement, regardless of the school environment, is going to be parental involvement.

B. **Subpoint:** This acknowledgement of parental involvement makes perfect sense. Parents have the responsibility to their children to empower them to succeed. They do not have to be the classroom teachers. What they do need to do, though, is be there for their children, no matter what kind of help is needed or situation arises. Parents need to support their children. They need to talk with them, and listen to them.

C. **Subpoint:** Problems in school are not uncommon. If parents are not hearing about these problems, it could be because they are not communicating effectively with their children. Parents need to keep communication lines open.

D. **Subpoint:** Even though it can be seen as a determinant for student success, parental involvement in no way justifies home schooling.

Conclusion

I. **Thesis restatement:** Without doubt, there is no reason to turn to home schooling as a complete alternative to our school systems.

156

II. **Main point summary:** Keep in mind the issues that I have addressed: parents' inadequacy as teachers, the best environment for learning, and the importance of parental involvement in schools.

III. **Clincher:** We need to put our children in the most effective schooling environment so that they can live up to their potential. If we truly want our children in the most effective classrooms for learning, and have the most effective teachers, then the home school is not where we want our children.

References

Ballman, R. (1995). *The how and why of home schooling.* Wheaton, Il: Crossway Books.

Colfax, D. M. (1987). *Homeschooling for excellence.* New York, NY: Mountain House Press.

Eisler, D. (1997). "Domestic lessons: Home-schoolers opt for a class of their own." *Maclean's,* 110, p. 64.

Hawkins, D. (1996, February 12). "Homeschool battles" [11 paragraphs]. U. S. News Online [Online]. Available at: http://www.usnews.com/usnews/issue/school.htm. (Version on December 1, 1997)

Mondloch, H. (2000). "Education hits home." *The World and I, 15,* p. 285–292.

Name _____ Section _____

Title of Speech _____

PREPARATION OUTLINE:
THE SPEECH OF POINT–COUNTERPOINT

Introduction

I.   Attention Step:

II. Listener Relevance Link:

III. Speaker Credibility:

IV. Thesis Statement:

V.   Preview of Speech:

Body

I.   First Main Point:

   A. Subpoint:

      1. Sub-Subpoint:

      2. Sub-Subpoint:

   B. Subpoint:

      1. Sub-Subpoint:

      2. Sub-Subpoint:

   Transition

II. Second Main Point:

   A. Subpoint:

      1. Sub-Subpoint:

      2. Sub-Subpoint:

   B. Subpoint:

      1. Sub-Subpoint:

      2. Sub-Subpoint:

   Transition:

III. Third Main Point:

   A. Subpoint:

         1. Sub-Subpoint:

         2. Sub-Subpoint:

      B. Subpoint:

         1. Sub-Subpoint:

         2. Sub-Subpoint:

Transition:

<u>Conclusion</u>

I.   **Thesis restatement:**

II. **Main point summary:**

III. **Clincher:**

<u>References</u>

List the references you used in the speech. Format them according to APA style (see Chapter 7 in your text for examples).

Name: _____ Section: _____

Title of Speech: _____

INSTRUCTOR CRITIQUE FORM
THE SPEECH OF POINT–COUNTERPOINT

Rating Scale 7 6 5 4 3 2 1
(Excellent)   (Poor)

Delivery	Critique	Points
Use of Voice: Intelligibility (rate, volume, pitch, quality, enunciation, pronunciation)? Conversational style? Fluency? Emotional expression (vocal variety, emotional conviction)?		
Use of Body: Attire? Poise (no distracting cues)? Eye contact? Facial Expression? Gestures? Motivated Movement? Initial and terminal ethos?		
Structure		
Macrostructure: Attention catcher? Listener Relevance? Speaker Credibility? Thesis statement? Preview? Transitions? Thesis restatement? Summary of main points? Clincher? "Clash?" Creativity?		
Microstructure: Language (clear, accuate, vivid, inclusive)? Persuasive "punch" words? Style (novelty, connectives, phrasing)? Technical jargon defined? No slang? No vocalized pauses (verbal garbage—"uh," "um," "like," "ya' know")?		
Content		
Analysis: Supporting points (appropriate, thematic, breadth, depth, listener relevance)? Rhetorical strategies (ethos, pathos, logos)? Appropriate focus? Learning styles? "Clash?"		
Supporting Material: Relevant? Recent? Varied? Credible? Clear? At least four? Distributed throughout? Properly credited? Presentational Aids (construction and integration)?		

Total Points: _____

Critic (your name): _____ Section: _____

Speaker (person you critiqued): _____

CLASSMATE CRITIQUE FORM
THE SPEECH OF POINT–COUNTERPOINT

Delivery	**CRITIQUE (Identify something the speaker did well and why. Identify something the speaker could do to improve, why, and how.)**
Use of Voice: Intelligibility (rate, volume, pitch, quality,enunciation, pronunciation)?Conversational style? Fluency? Emotional expression (vocal variety, emotional conviction)?	
Use of Body: Attire? Poise (no distracting cues)? Eye contact? Facial Expression? Gestures? Motivated Movement? Initial and terminal ethos?	

Structure	**CRITIQUE (Identify something the speaker did well and why. Identify something the speaker could do to improve, why, and how.)**
Macrostructure: Attention catcher? Listener Relevance? Speaker Credibility? Thesis statement? Preview? Transitions? Thesis restatement? Summary of main points? Clincher? "Clash?" Creativity?	
Microstructure: Language (clear, accuate, vivid, inclusive)? Persuasive "punch" words? Style (novelty, connectives, phrasing)? Technical jargon defined? No Slang? No vocalized pauses?	

Content	**CRITIQUE (Identify something the speaker did well and why. Identify something the speaker could do to improve, why, and how.)**
Analysis: Supporting points (appropriate, thematic, breadth, depth, listener relevance)? Rhetorical strategies (ethos, pathos, logos)? Appropriate focus? Learning styles? "Clash?"	
Supporting Material: Relevant? Recent? Varied? Credible? Clear? At least four? Distributed throughout? Properly credited? Presentational Aids?	

Name:_____Section:_____

SELF-CRITIQUE FORM:
THE POINT-COUNTERPOINT SPEECH

Goal: To evaluate your own performance.

Rationale: As a form of cognitive restructuring, this exercise can help reduce public speaking anxiety while it helps you improve as a public speaker.

Directions: (a) In groups of 4 to 6 students, discuss your last speech performance based on the following guidelines. Then, complete and turn in this form based on your thoughts and the group discussion. OR (b) Watch a videotape of yourself giving your last speech. Complete this form and turn it in.

1. In terms of **Delivery,** the requirements for this speech were to sound intelligible, conversational, and express emotional conviction; and to look poised, wear appropriate attire, use effective eye contact, facial expression, gestures, motivated movement; and to convey initial and terminal ethos. I did the following things well in my last speech:

a.

b.

2. In terms of **Content,** the requirements were to be within the time constraint; offer ethos, pathos, and logos; round the cycle of learning, and offer depth, breadth and listener relevance; cite at least four external sources, and "clash" with my partner. I did the following things well in my last speech:

a.

b.

3. In terms of **Structure,** the requirements were to offer all macrostructural elements in a creative way that "clashes" with my partner, use clear, inclusive, colorful language, use persuasive "punch" words, use no slang or verbal garbage, and use style in connectives and phrasing. I did the following things well in my last speech:

a.

b.

4. If I could do my last speech over again, I would do the following things differently:

a.

b.

c.

5. Overall, I would give myself a grade of _____ on my last speech because . . .

6. To improve as a public speaker on my next speech, I am going to try to:

a.

b.

Name _____

POINT–COUNTERPOINT SPEECH
LISTENER SELF-REFLECTION

Goal: To understand why you were or were not persuaded to accept a speaker's position.

Rationale: This assignment will help you understand the persuasive strategies that most effectively "speak" to you as a listener.

Directions: Take a few moments to answer each of the following questions.

1. Which speaker's argument did you agree more with after listening?

2. Did you already have an opinion about this issue before listening? What was that opinion?

3. List three specific examples offered in the speeches that influenced you to "vote for" the argument you identified in question #1.

   a.

   b.

   c.

4. Identify examples of ethos pathos and logos offered by the speaker whose argument you identified in question #1.

    a. ETHOS:

    b. PATHOS:

    c. LOGOS:

5. Which rhetorical strategy was most influential for YOU as a listener and why?

ACTUATION PERSUASIVE SPEECHES

Actuation persuasive speeches attempt to change the behavior of individuals or some group in society. The thesis statement is formulated around a claim of policy.

ORGANIZATIONAL FORMATS

You will use one of four organizational formats for this speech. These formats are Problem–Cause–Solution, Monroe's Motivated Sequence, problem/solution, and modified comparative advantages.

In the problem–cause–solution format, you use these three areas each as one of your main points. For the first main point, you talk about the problem. Here you reveal the propensity of the problem. How widespread is it (or could it be)? How many people are affected (or could be affected) by it? You also reveal the depth of the problem in the first main point. To what degree are people afflicted by it? Do they die? How devastating are the effects of the problem? In the second main point, you talk about the cause (or causes) of the problem. Here you talk about why the problem exists. What factors are causing this problem to occur? Identify as many causes (contributors) as you can generate. The third main point is where you offer solutions to the problem. Solutions are usually identified on a broad (national or international) level, a local (cities, communities, and organizations) level, and a personal level (what each person in the room ought to do to help solve the problem. Your clincher for this speech is a call to action step urging audience members to take action, to do their part to solve the problem.

In Monroe's Motivated Sequence, you talk about similar issues in a little bit different format. In your first main point, you talk about the need for a change. You point to a problem that exists and identify why the problem needs to be changed. In your second main point, you pose a plan (or plans) for eliminating the need. In your third main point, you visualize the future. You attempt to describe what the future will look like if the plan is not implemented (negative visualization) and if the plan is implemented (positive visualization). Your clincher for this speech is a call to action step urging audience members to take action, to do their part to solve the problem.

If you decide to use problem/solution or modified comparative advantages, you should consult Chapters 15 and 16 in the text and talk to your instructor.

PROBLEM–CAUSE–SOLUTION
GENERIC OUTLINE

(Actuation Persuasive Speech Format)

Introduction

I. **Attention Catcher**

II. **Listener Relevance**

III. **Speaker Credibility**

IV. **Thesis statement**

V. **Preview**   In this speech, your main points will always consist of the problem, the cause(s), and the solution.

Body

I. **First Main Point—The Problem**

Here is where you talk about the significance of the problem. Who does it affect? How many people are affected? How does it affect them? To what degree are they affected?

A. Subpoints are developed with specific instances (examples).

B. Subpoints are developed with facts and statistics.

C. Subpoints are developed by relating the problem to the audience members (listener relevance).

Transition:

II. **Second Main Point—The Cause(s)**

Here is where you talk about what factors are contributing to creation of the problem. Why does the problem exist? What are the things that would have to change in order to eliminate the problem?

A. Subpoints are developed with specific instances (examples).

B. Subpoints are developed with facts and statistics.

Subpoints are developed by relating the problem to the audience members (listener relevance).

Transition:

III. **Third Main Point—The Solution(s)**

Here is where you offer the solutions to the problem. You may discuss places where the solution has worked before. You may explain why it will help solve the problem because it eradicates one of the causes of the problem.

A. National or International level (What should the government do to help solve the problem?)

B. Local level (What should states, communities, organizations do to help solve the problem?)

C. Personal level (What should each person in the room do to help solve the problem?)

Conclusion

I. **Thesis restatement**

II. **Main point summary**

III. **Call to Action/Clincher:** Request specific action from the audience. State your personal intent to take the same course of action requested of your listeners. Recapture interest in a way that ties back to the attention catcher.

References

MONROE'S MOTIVATED SEQUENCE
GENERIC OUTLINE
(Actuation Persuasive Speech Format)

Introduction

I. **Attention Catcher**

II. **Listener Relevance Link**

III. **Speaker Credibility**

IV. **Thesis Statement**

V. **Preview.** In this speech, your main points will always consist of the need step, the satisfaction step, and the visualization step.

Body

I. **First Main Point—Need Step**

There are potentially two kinds of needs from which to choose. For your speech, you will choose either "need for a change" (point out what's wrong with present conditions) or "need to preserve present conditions" (point out the dangers which may result from impending change).

A. Subpoints are developed in the following ways:

Illustration—Reveal one or more incidents to illustrate the need.

Ramifications—Employ as many additional facts, examples, and quotations as are required to make the need convincingly impressive.

Pointing—Illuminate the importance of this issue to audience members.

Transition

II. **Second Main Point—Satisfaction Step**

This step satisfies the need by presenting a workable solution to eliminate the need.

A. Subpoints are developed in the following ways:

Explanation—State your proposal in an easily understood fashion.

Theoretical demonstration—Show how the solution logically and adequately meets the need pointed out in the need step. Develop this segment thoroughly.

Practical Experience—Cite actual examples of where this proposal has worked effectively.

Meeting Objections—Forestall opposition by showing how your proposal over-comes any objections that might arise.

Transition

III. Third Main Point—Visualization Step

The visualization step must attempt to stand the test of reality. The conditions you describe must seem realistic. The more vividly you describe the projected situation, the stronger reaction it will evoke from the audience.

A. Subpoints may be developed from three methods of visualizing the future.

Positive Visualization—Describe the conditions as they will exist in the future if your proposal solution is actually implemented. Picture your listeners enjoying the safety, pleasure, or pride that acceptance of your proposal will have produced.

Negative Visualization—Describe the conditions of the future if your proposed solution is not carried out. Picture the audience enduring the unpleasant effects resulting from their failure to implement your proposal.

Contrasting Visualization—In this method, you combine positive and negative visualization. Begin by illustrating negative visualization (undesirable future results) and conclude by illuminating positive visualization (desirable future results).

Conclusion

I. **Thesis restatement**

II. **Main point summary**

III. **Call to Action/Clincher.** Request specific action from the audience. State your personal intent to take the same course of action requested of your listeners. Recapture interest in a way which ties back to the attention catcher.

References

THE ACTUATION PERSUASIVE SPEECH
(by an individual)

Description: This is a 8- to 10-minute actuation persuasive speech. In other words, you must attempt to change behavior and solve some problem in the world. You might address a global problem, national problem, local problem, or campus problem. Your thesis statement is formulated around a question of policy. You will use one of four organizational formats for this speech. These formats are: Problem/Solution, Problem–Cause–Solution, Modified Comparative Advantages, or Monroe's Motivated Sequence (Chapter 15 in the textbook). Lectern is required for this speech as is the use of PowerPoint presentational aids. Points will be deducted for going over or under the time limits, for not using a *speaking outline* (key words and phrases), or for using more than five 3 × 5 inch index cards (one side only).

Rationale: This speech requires PowerPoint presentational aids and at least 6 external sources distributed throughout. Since it is most difficult to successfully incite behavioral changes and policy changes, it is crucial to use as many tools to enhance ethos, pathos, and logos as possible.

GRADING CRITERIA
ACTUATION PERSUASIVE SPEECH
Individual (49 points)

Delivery

Use of Voice:
- Intelligible, conversational, and sincere.
- Fluency.
- Emotional Expression. You should sound committed to your opinions about the issue. You need to have *emotional conviction* in your voice or you will never convince your audience to share your opinion or move them to action.

Use of Body:
- Attire, poise, and eye contact.
- Facial expression, gestures, and motivated movement.
- Initial and terminal ethos (conveyed with pauses at the beginning and end of speech).

Structure

Macrostructure:
- All elements must be clearly articulated.
- Creativity. Use organizational format that lends itself to persuasion (problem/solution, problem/cause/solution, Monroe's Motivated Sequence).

Microstructure:
- Inclusive, concrete, jargon defined, no slang, very few vocalized pauses.
- Language. Use persuasive "punch" words in structural comments to enhance pathos.
- Style. And use phrasing that enhances pathos.

Content

Analysis/Reasoning:
- Be descriptive and within the time constraint.
- Listener relevance must be addressed for each main point.
- Ethos, pathos, and logos must be evident.
- Learning styles must all be addressed.

Supporting Materials:
- You must cite at least three oral footnotes from different sources during the speech. These sources must be varied, credible to your topic, distributed throughout the speech, and properly credited.
- Evidence. You must use different kinds of supporting material as evidence throughout your speech (examples, analogies, testimonies, surveys, facts, statistics, etc.).

PowerPoint Presentational Aids:
- Constructed according to guidelines for effective presentational aids.
- Integrated according to guidelines for effective presentational aids.

ACTUATION PERSUASIVE SPEECH EXAMPLE
Problem–Cause–Solution Design

Formal Outline: "Domestic Violence"
Amanda Brown

Introduction

I. **Attention Catcher:** According to Old English Law, it was legal for a man to beat his wife with a stick or rod, which was no bigger around than his thumb. This law became known as "the rule of thumb." This law may seem old and archaic, but its effects can still be seen today.

II. **Listener Relevance:** We will never be sure how many people, especially women, are impacted by domestic violence. But, the Department of Justice, cited in the February 1999 edition of *Sex Roles*, estimates the number to be at least one million per year. This could include an acquaintance, someone close to you, or you.

III. **Speaker Credibility:** I have done extensive research in the area of domestic violence and, thus, feel qualified to speak to you regarding the topic.

IV. **Thesis:** Action must be taken to reduce domestic violence.

V. **Preview:** To help you see why this is so important, let's examine the scope of the problem, unearth some of its underlying causes, and finally present some possible solutions we should enact to curb the pervasive problem of domestic violence.

Body

I. **First Main Point (Problem):** Domestic violence is a much bigger problem than many people realize.

   A. **Subpoint (Listener Relevance):** We've all heard the saying "out of sight, out of mind," and the same holds true for domestic violence. Because the problem is highly underreported, especially among men, the public never really knows the extent of domestic violence.

   B. **Subpoint:** Most estimates of domestic violence are conservative, due to underreporting of the crime. According to a report by the Surgeon General, published in the book *Helping Survivors of Domestic Violence*, 21–34% of all women will be assaulted by a male partner in their lifetime. That is 1/5 to 1/3 of all women.

   C. **Subpoint:** In addition to a significant amount of people being abused, the same Surgeon General study, cited above, stated that domestic violence is the number one cause of emergency room visits by women. In fact, 1/3 to ___ of all acute emergency room visits are a result of domestic violence.

   D. **Subpoint:** Finally, the media is a significant contributor to domestic violence. Julia Wood, in her book *Gendered Lives*, argued the media represent men and women stereotypically. Men are portrayed as strong and hyper-masculine, while women are represented as submissive, weak, and reliant upon men.

Transition: Few would argue with the claim that domestic violence is a bad thing. However, there is less agreement as to what are the core causes of it.

II. **Second Main Point (Causes):** There are numerous causes of domestic violence.

   A. **Subpoint (Listener Relevance):** Human beings are naturally curious. We want to know how things work and why things happen. Domestic violence is no different and its causes have been debated for years.

   B. **Subpoint:** One of the most pervasive causes of domestic violence is patriarchy, or the belief men should be in control. According to volume 61 of the *Journal of Consulting and Clinical Psychology*, men often resort to violence to gain power over women when they feel subordinate and want to gain power over women.

   C. **Subpoint:** In addition to patriarchy, there are many misconceptions regarding domestic violence.

      1. **Sub-Subpoint:** There is the perception that alcohol, drugs, or a lack of money are the cause of domestic violence.

      2. **Sub-Subpoint:** Also, there is the view women enjoy the abuse and that is why they stay in the abusive relationship. In fact, the book *Reconstructing Political Theory* explained 90% of abused women would leave if resources, such as housing, employment, and safety from their abusive partner were available to them.

      3. **Sub-Subpoint:** Finally, the media skew our perceptions of domestic violence. Marian Meyers, in the Spring 1994 *Journal of Communication*, stated the media distort the image of domestic violence. It is shown as impacting poor, black women disproportionately. In fact, domestic violence transcends race, religion, and socioeconomic status.

Transition: Unfortunately, a tolerance of domestic violence is ingrained in our society. But, luckily, there are solutions to the problem.

III. **Third Main Point (Solutions):** There are solutions to domestic violence.

   A. **Subpoint (Listener Relevance):** Not only are we curious, we also seek fast and easy solutions to our problems. While there is no panacea for domestic violence, there are steps that can be taken to reduce the problem.

   B. **Subpoint:** To begin combating domestic violence, there must be a shift in the focus from the victim to the abuser. Unfortunately, for someone to escape domestic violence, they must give up their home, their career, split up their family, and hide from their abuser, while the abuser is free.

   C. **Subpoint:** Next, the media need to present less stereotypical images of men and women. As Julia Wood, cited above, argued, the media are gatekeepers of information. Not only do the media reflect what is happening in society, but they also shape what society thinks about certain issues.

   D. **Subpoint:** Finally, there are steps each one of us can take.

      1. **Sub-Subpoint:** We must learn all we can about domestic violence so we can avoid making false judgments about the problem and its victims.

      2. **Sub-Subpoint:** Also, we must boycott television programs and films that rely on stereotypical images of men and women and domestic violence.

      3. **Sub-Subpoint:** And, we must let networks know we are upset when they portray domestic violence.

Conclusion

I. **Thesis restatement:** Without doubt, domestic violence is indeed a problem that must be addressed.

II. **Main point summary:** Specifically, we examined the scope of the problem, several of its underlying causes, and posed some workable solutions.

III. **Clincher:** Let me leave you with this thought. The next time you hear someone talking about his or her "rule of thumb," you know the true meaning of the cliché. And, while domestic violence is a prominent part of our past, it does not have to be part of our future.

References

Babcock, J.C., Walz, J., Jacobson, N.J. and Gottman, J.M. (1993). Power and violence: the relation between communication patterns, power discrepancies, and domestic violence. *Journal of consulting and clinical psychology*, 61, 40-50.

Gordon, J.S. (1998). *Helping survivors of domestic violence: The effectives of medial, mental health, and community services*. New York: Garland Publishing, Inc.

Locke, L.M. (1999). Attitudes toward domestic violence: Race and gender issues. *Sex roles*, 40, 3-20.

Meyers, M. (1994). News of battering. *Journal of communication*, 44, 47-63.

Shanley, M.L. and Narayan, U. (Eds.) (1997). *Reconstructing political theory: Feminist perspectives*. University Park, PA: The University Press.

Wood, J. (1994). *Gendered lives: Communication, gender and culture*. Belmont, CA: Wadsworth.

ACTUATION PERSUASIVE SPEECH EXAMPLE
Problem–Cause–Solution Design

Formal Outline: "Teen Suicide"

Peter Klemin

Introduction

I.   **Attention Catcher:** Julie was sitting on the swing in her back yard crying. She had just returned from a big party where her boyfriend Tommy had just dumped her. It seemed like everything was going wrong these days. She was failing her classes, her friends acted too cool for her, and her parents just kept yelling at her to straighten out. The only problem was that she couldn't, so Julie swallowed a handful of pills and never woke up.

II. **Listener Relevance:** Many of you probably had troubles similar to Julie, and some of you may have known a person that took the final leap like Julie.

III **Speaker Credibility:** I don't have any personal experiences with teen suicide, but I do have a deep concern for teens that want to end their lives.

IV. **Thesis:** Teen suicide is a serious problem today; one we must no longer ignore.

V.   **Preview:** To help convince you, I will first offer some startling statistics about teen suicide. Second, I will reveal several causes for teen suicide. Third, I will pose several solutions we can implement to prevent teen suicide.

   Transition: I would like to begin by giving you some horrifying stats on teen suicide.

Body

I.   **First Main Point:** The numbers of teens committing suicide these days is horrendous.

   Listener Relevance: I'm sure that many of you have heard in classes, on the news, or read in the papers how prevalent teen suicide is.

   A. **Subpoint:** According to a December 1997 article in *Current Health* magazine, Janice Arenofsky said teen suicide is the third leading cause of adolescent death. One out of four high school kids seriously considers suicide.

   B. **Subpoint:** In his 1971 book, *Adolescent Suicide*, Jerry Jacobs wrote that teen suicide was the fifth leading cause of adolescent death. That means that teen suicide is four times more common today than it was 20 years ago.

   Transition: Although the numbers are fairly simple, the causes of suicide are varied.

II. **Second Main Point:** The causes for teen suicide not only vary from person to person, but also from year to year.

   Listener Relevance: Many parents have said to their kids that growing up was different for them, just as reasons for suicide are different for our generation.

A. **Subpoint:** In a June 1967 article in the *Saturday Evening Post*, Max Gunther wrote that fear of punishment or an overwhelming downfall in sex or school were leading reasons for teen suicide in that era.

B. **Subpoint:** According to Arenofsky's *Current Health* article, depression is the leading cause today. Depression caused by obesity, physical differences, low self-esteem, and questions about sexual orientation. Today, more and more teens also have to face issues of divorce, death, abuse, pregnancy, and stress.

Transition: Because these problems are not impossible to overcome, we can take steps to prevent teen suicide.

III. **Third Main Point:** All of us have the ability to help prevent teen suicide.

Listener Relevance: The loss of a friend or loved one to suicide would be devastating to us all. It is important that we know what to do when we see this situation.

A. **Subpoint:** On the Suicide Awareness/Voices of Education (SAVE) website, accessed on October 10, 1999, this organization stated that knowing the signs of depression is very important because it is the leading cause of teen suicide today.

B. **Subpoint:** These signs include pessimism, sadness, irritability, helplessness, and talking about death. The SAVE organization recommends that we find help for the teen. They recommend that you talk to a parent, counselor, doctor, teacher, and/or clergy.

C. **Subpoint:** Listening is also important. SAVE recommends: really listening, reassuring the teen, don't judge the teen's reasons, and don't keep the suicide threat a secret—tell someone.

Conclusion

I. **Thesis restatement:** Today, I told you about the frightening trend of teen suicide.

II. **Main point summary:** I have given you some stats about teen suicide, causes of teen suicide, and ways to help prevent teen suicide.

III. **Clincher:** Julie had problems, but she didn't seek help or receive any help. So, please, if you know someone that is having a tough time in their life, help them or find someone who can.

References

Arenofsky, J. (1997). Teen suicide: when the blues get out of control. *Current Health*, pp. 16–18.

Gunther, M. (1967). Why children commit suicide. *The Saturday Evening Post*, 240, pp. 86–89.

Jacobs, J. (1971). *Adolescent Suicide*. New York, NY: Wiley-Interscience.

Suicide Awareness/Voices of Education. [online]. SAVE. Available at: http://www.save.org.html. [1999, October 10].

Name _____ Section _____

Title of Speech _____

PREPARATION OUTLINE
THE ACTUATION PERSUASIVE SPEECH BY AN INDIVIDUAL

Introduction

I.   **Attention Step:**

II. **Listener Relevance Link:**

III. **Speaker Credibility:**

IV. **Thesis Statement:**

V.   **Preview:**

Body

I.   **First Main Point:**

   A. Subpoint:

      1. Sub-Subpoint:

      2. Sub-Subpoint:

   B. Subpoint:

      1. Sub-Subpoint:

      2. Sub-Subpoint:

   Transition:

II. **Second Main Point:**

   A. Subpoint:

      1. Sub-Subpoint:

      2. Sub-Subpoint:

   B. Subpoint:

      1. Sub-Subpoint:

      2. Sub-Subpoint:

Transition:

III. **Third Main Point:**

    A. Subpoint:

        1. Sub-Subpoint:

        2. Sub-Subpoint:

    B. Subpoint:

        1. Sub-Subpoint:

        2. Sub-Subpoint:

Transition:

Conclusion

I.   **Thesis restatement:**

II. **Main point summary:**

III. **Clincher:**

References

List the references you used in the speech. Format them according to APA style (see Chapter 7 in your text for examples).

Name: _____ Section: _____

Title of Speech: _____

INSTRUCTOR CRITIQUE FORM
The Actuation Persuasive Speech (Individual)

Rating Scale   7   6   5   4   3   2   1
                 (Excellent)   (Poor)

Individual Grade	Critique	Points
Delivery		
Use of Voice: Intelligibility? Conversational style? Fluency? Emotional expression? (variety and conviction)?		
Use of Body: Attire? Poise? Eye contact? Facial Expression? Gestures? Use of lectern?		
Structure		
Macrostructure: Attention Catcher? Listener Relevance? Speaker Credibility? Thesis? Preview? Transitions? Thesis Restatement? Main Point Summary? Clincher? Creativity?		
Microstructure: Language (clear, accurate, VIVID, Inclusive)? Style (Novelty, connectives, phrasing)? Jargon? Slang? Vocalized pauses?		
Content		
Analysis: Thematic? Focus, (time constraint)? Breadth? Depth? Listener Relevance? Rhetorical Strategies? Learning Styles?		
Supporting Material: Relevant? Recent? Varied? Credible? Distributed throughout? Properly Credited? At least four?		
PowerPoint Visual Aid: Construction? Integration?		

Total Points: _____

Critic (your name): _____ Section: _____

Speaker (person you critiqued): _____

CLASSMATE CRITIQUE FORM
The Actuation Persuasive Speech by an Individual

Delivery	**CRITIQUE** (Identify something the speaker did well and why. Identify something the speaker could do to improve, why, and how.)
Use of Voice: Intelligibility (rate, volume, pitch, quality,enunciation, pronunciation)? Conversational style? Fluency? Emotional expression (vocal variety, emotional conviction)?	
Use of Body: Attire? Poise (no distracting cues)? Eye contact? Facial Expression? Gestures? Motivated Movement? Initial and terminal ethos?	

Structure	**CRITIQUE** (Identify something the speaker did well and why. Identify something the speaker could do to improve, why, and how.)
Macrostructure: Attention catcher? Listener Relevance? Speaker Credibility? Thesis statement? Preview? Transitions? Thesis restatement? Summary of main points? Clincher? "Clash?" Creativity?	
Microstructure: Language (clear, accuate, vivid, inclusive, colorful)? Persuasive "punch" words? Style (novelty, connectives, phrasing)? Technical jargon defined? No Slang? No vocalized pauses?	

Content	**CRITIQUE** (Identify something the speaker did well and why. Identify something the speaker could do to improve, why, and how.)
Analysis: Supporting points (accurate, varied, depth, related to thesis)? Rhetorical strategies (ethos, pathos, logos)? Appropriate focus? Listener Relevance? Learning styles? Call to action?	
Supporting Material: Relevant? Recent? Varied? Credible? Clear? Distributed throughout? Properly credited? At least four?	
Presentational Aids? Construction? Integration?	

Name:_____Section:_____

SELF-CRITIQUE FORM:
THE ACTUATION PERSUASIVE SPEECH

Goal: To evaluate your own performance.

Rationale: As a form of cognitive restructuring, this exercise can help reduce public speaking anxiety while it helps you improve as a public speaker.

Directions: (a) In groups of 4 to 6 students, discuss your last speech performance based on the following guidelines. Then, complete and turn in this form based on your thoughts and the group discussion. OR (b) Watch a videotape of yourself giving your last speech. Complete this form and turn it in.

1. In terms of **Delivery,** the requirements for this speech were to sound intelligible, conversational, and express emotional conviction; and to look poised, wear appropriate attire, use effective eye contact, facial expression, gestures, motivated movement; and to convey initial and terminal ethos. I did the following things well in my last speech:

a.

b.

2. In terms of **Content,** the requirements were to be within the time constraint; offer ethos, pathos, and logos; round the cycle of learning, and offer depth, breadth and listener relevance; cite at least four external sources, and a clear call to action. I did the following things well in my last speech:

a.

b.

3. In terms of **Structure,** the requirements were to offer all macrostructural elements in a creative way, use clear, inclusive, colorful language, use persuasive "punch" words, use no slang or verbal garbage, and use style in connectives and phrasing. I did the following things well in my last speech:

a.

b.

4. In terms of my **PowerPoint Presentational Aids,** the requirements were to construct them well and integrate them effectively. I did the following things well in my last speech:

a.

b.

186

5. If I could do my last speech over again, I would do the following things differently:

a.

b.

c.

6. Overall, I would give myself a grade of _____ on my last speech because . . .

7. To improve as a public speaker on my next speech, I am going to try to:

a.

b.

ACTUATION PERSUASIVE SYMPOSIUM SPEECH

Goal: To prepare and present an actuation persuasive speech in a group.

Rationale: The business world is requiring more and more teamwork skills of their employees. This may involve working effectively in groups as well as speaking effectively in groups. This assignment provides students an opportunity to critique the ethical membership practices of one another while preparing an actuation symposium speech. Students must work effectively in a team to prepare and present an effective speech. They also must present visual aids using PowerPoint multimedia technology, which will be directly applicable to them if their careers should be in business and industry.

SPEAKING IN A SYMPOSIUM

Description: Your objective in this speaking assignment is to participate with 4 to 6 classmates in the process of sharing information on a topic for an audience. Each of you must prepare and deliver a speech on a specific segment of the more general topic chosen for the symposium. Your group should select a topic which is of interest to the membership of your group and to your listeners. The symposium offers the listener an extended and in-depth treatment of a topic. While symposiums are freqently informative in nature, the group will add a persuasive component to the presentation. The group will divide a general topic into specific sub-topic areas and will present their remarks in an assigned speaking order.

Special Requirements: Each of you, as a member of the symposium, will examine at least 2 to 3 different sources in the process of preparing your speech. The format of your speech will follow that which is used for a persuasive speech. You are expected to have an introduction, body, and conclusion to the speech. The format will either be Monroe's Motivated Sequence or some form of the Problem–Cause–Solution format. Each of the group members who have to speak on one of the main points must have their own miniature speech format with an introduction, body, and conclusion of their own. If there are more than 4 people, the group must decide who will do what. Your group will need to choose one person to serve as the moderator of the symposium. Most often, the moderator gives either the introduction or the conclusion or both. The moderator will introduce each of you and your topic when providing transitions between speakers. PowerPoint will be used for the group's visual aids. Each person must utilize at least one slide in their speech. Each slide must have one nonverbal symbol system (pie chart, line graph, or a diagram) that visually helps the listener understand the message. One typed outline for the entire group speech will be turned in on rehearsal day. The time limit for the symposium is 15 to 20 minutes, and individual speeches consisting of each main point must be 4 to 6 minutes in length.

GRADING CRITERIA
ACTUATION PERSUASIVE SYMPOSIUM SPEECH
Individual (28 points)

Delivery

Use of Voice:
- Intelligible, conversational, and sincere.
- Fluency.
- Emotional Expression. You should sound committed to your opinions about the issue. You need to have *emotional conviction* in your voice or you will never convince your audience to share your opinion or move them to action.

Use of Body:
- Attire, poise, and eye contact.
- Facial expression, gestures, and motivated movement.
- Initial and terminal ethos (conveyed with pauses at the beginning and end of speech).

Structure

Macrostructure:
- All elements must be clearly articulated.
- Creativity. Use organizational format that lends itself to persuasion (problem/solution, problem/cause/solution, Monroe's Motivated Sequence).

Microstructure:
- Inclusive, concrete, jargon defined, no slang, very few vocalized pauses.
- Language. Use persuasive "punch" words in structural comments to enhance pathos.
- Style. And use phrasing that enhances pathos.

Content

Analysis/Reasoning:
- Be descriptive and within the time constraint (as in the Speech of Personal Significance).
- Listener relevance must be addressed for each main point.
- Ethos, pathos, and logos must be evident.
- Learning styles must all be addressed.

Supporting Materials:
- You must cite at least three oral footnotes from different sources during the speech. These sources must be varied, credible to your topic, distributed throughout the speech, and properly credited.
- Evidence. You must use different kinds of supporting material as evidence throughout your speech (examples, analogies, testimonies, surveys, facts, statistics, etc.).

PowerPoint Presentational Aids:
- Constructed according to guidelines for effective presentational aids.
- Integrated according to guidelines for effective presentational aids.

GRADING CRITERIA
ACTUATION PERSUASIVE SYMPOSIUM SPEECH
Group (21 points)

Dynamics

- Based on group dynamics peer critiques, evaluations, and reflection papers.
- Teamwork?
- Cooperation?
- Synergy?

Content

- Thematic?
- Appropriate focus?
- Substance? Thorough coverage of topic areas?
- Supporting material (recent, relevant, varied, distributed throughout — at least two by each speaker, properly credited)
- Rhetorical strategies (ethos, pathos, logos)?
- Learning styles?

PowerPoint

- Thematic slide layout, transitions, background designs?
- Constructed effectively?
- Integrated effectively?

ACTUATION PERSUASIVE SYMPOSIUM SPEECH EXAMPLE
Monroe's Motivated Sequence Design

Formal Outline: "The Dirty Truth about Antibacterial Products"
Jennifer Gilderhus, Megan Gilderhus, Stephanie Ahlfeldt, and Daniel Grothues

Introduction

I. **Attention Catcher:** A meticulously dressed man in a suit and overcoat squeezed his way through the rush-hour crowd as he boarded the New York City subway. As he braced himself for the ride ahead, he noticed a sign above him that read, "You are the 423rd person to touch that pole today!" Nearby another advertisement warned, "The last guy to touch that pole was named Sal Monella."

II. **Listener Relevance:** Just think of the hundreds of people who have sat in that very seat, touched that same spot in front of you. How many of those people did not wash their hands in the bathroom before sitting there?

III. **Speaker Credibility:** Through our research, we have found that America's obsession with germs is being fueled by misleading advertising and overzealous use of antibacterial products.

IV. **Thesis:** Americans' overuse of antibacterial products is reducing their effectiveness as germ fighters.

V. **Preview:** Today we're going to get down and dirty with germs. Jennifer Gilderhus will be the moderator. Megan Gilderhus will identify the abuse of antibacterial products and will describe its dangerous results, Daniel Grothues will propose a more practical solution for germ removal, and Stephanie Ahlfeldt will visualize a continued future of antibacterial overuse. Together, we will propose a more realistic approach for germ protection; one that includes the practical use of antibacterial products.

Transition: Most of us have heard of these products, many of us buy them and use them regularly. Megan will begin by telling us why these products are not as effective as we would like them to be.

Body

I. **First Main Point (Need–Problem):** Americans are overusing antibacterial products.

   Listener Relevance: You might be familiar with the way a disk jockey overplays a new song on the radio. After a few days, you are tired of hearing the same songs over and over. In that same way, Americans are overusing antibacterial products.

   A. **Subpoint:** We are obsessed with being clean and will buy any product that promises complete germ removal.

      1. **Sub-Subpoint:** The May 9, 1999 edition of the *Washington Post* reports on how one lady's obsession with being clean led her to buy an antibacterial pizza cutter and Calvin Klein antibacterial socks!

      2. **Sub-Subpoint:** One in five Americans has a family member who is obsessed with germs. (Rosin, 1997, p. On-line).

3. **Sub-Subpoint:** 39% of Americans said they have changed their cleaning habits due to germs. (Rosin, 1997, p. On-line).

4. **Sub-Subpoint:** Last year alone, retailers sold $400 million worth of antibacterial products. (Rosin, 1999, p. On-line).

B. **Subpoint:** Antibacterial product advertising creates a false sense of security.

1. **Sub-Subpoint:** A recent survey conducted for the Infectious Diseases Society of America found that nearly half of all soaps on the market now contain antibacterial agents (Leland, 2000, p. On-line).

2. **Sub-Subpoint:** According to Dr. Student Levy of Tufts University, "At best these products are ineffective. Even if one did work when first applied, as its level of concentration dropped, bacteria could produce strains that resist it," (Leland, 2000, p. On-line).

3. **Sub-Subpoint:** In response to this threat, the American Medical Association suggested government regulation for antibacterial products. (Leland, 2000, p. On-line).

Transition: Thank you Megan for highlighting some of the problems with antibacterial products. Please continue by bringing to our attention the consequences of our overuse.

II. **Second Main Point (Need–Cause):** An effect of antibacterial product overuse is reduced effectiveness.

Listener Relevance: None of us like to feel dirty – especially Americans. That's why we take showers or baths, wear cologne and perfume and buy hundreds of products that will make us smell better and feel cleaner.

A. **Subpoint:** Overuse of antibacterial products may increase illness and bring on new germs.

1. **Sub-Subpoint:** There is a growing contention that we don't have enough dirt and germs in our lives. (Leland, 2000, p. On-line).

2. **Sub-Subpoint:** According the September 12, 2000 Minneapolis *Star Tribune*, a few studies show that this crusade for cleanliness may have gone too far. Researchers believe our progress in domestic hygiene may be responsible for the increased rates of asthma, eczema, hayfever, and allergies and many open the venue for new germs.

3. **Sub-Subpoint:** As Dr. Andrew Liu, pediatric asthma specialist at the National Jewish Medical Research Center in Denver states in the aforementioned *Tribune* article, "We're finding that childhood exposure to infections and certain environmental toxins seems to have a protective effect."

B. **Subpoint:** Bacteria are showing signs of resistance to antibacterial agents.

1. **Sub-Subpoint:** New studies are showing that more and more bacteria are becoming impervious to antibacterial agents in "germ killing" soaps and cleansers. (Kolata, 2001, p. On-line).

2. **Sub-Subpoint:** Popular antibacterial hand soaps provide extra protection, but they do not sterilize hands and they are not approved by the FDA. (Davis, 1999, p. On-line).

Transition: As Megan has described, our overuse is a serious problem. Daniel will now propose a more practical solution for germ control.

III. **Third Main Point (Satisfaction–Solution):** Our suggestion for practical germ protection is three-fold. Consumer awareness, moderated use of antibacterial products, and proper hygiene practices are the focus of our solution.

Listener Relevance: I'm sure almost all of us have bought a product because of cool labeling or an attractive advertisement. We can still feel clean and avoid unsightly germs by being more alert to product advertising

A. **Subpoint:** Antibacterial product advertising promises much more than most products can produce.

    1. **Sub-Subpoint:** The first thing to know is that many scientists and government officials have complained that the advertising on these products is misleading, and the Environmental Protection Agency has disciplined several companies for exaggerated claims. (Rosin, 1999, p. On-line).

    2. **Sub-Subpoint:** Hasbro advertised that its antibacterial toys and highchairs "protect your child from germs and bacteria." The EPA made Hasbro change the claim after it was found untrue. (Rosin, 1999, p. On-line).

B. **Subpoint:** If you do use antibacterial products, use them in moderation.

    1. **Sub-Subpoint:** We've gone overboard trying to kill everything in the environment. (Kolata, 2001, p. On-line)

    2. **Sub-Subpoint:** As a result, the Federal Trade Commission has begun cracking down on germ-fighting claims being made for a growing number of antibacterial products. (Mayer, 1999, p. On-line)

    3. **Sub-Subpoint:** Jodie Bernstein, Director of the FTC's Bureau of Consumer Protection says, "the message we hope to send consumers is 'Don't think that these products give you any better protection than washing your hands with soap and hot water.' " (Mayer, 1999, p. On-line)

C. **Subpoint:** For practical germ removal, the solution is simple.

    1. **Sub-Subpoint:** Handwashing. This is the tip mentioned first by everyone. It sounds simple, but it is still the best way to prevent infection. (Burcum, 2000, p. On-line)

    2. **Sub-Subpoint:** However, doing it correctly is important. The U.S. Centers for Disease Control and Prevention recommends this process: wet hands with warm soap and water, lather up with soap, rub hands together briskly for 10 seconds, rinse, and dry off with a paper towel. (Burcum, 2000, p. On-line)

Transition: Dr. Marc Micozzi, chairman of the National Hygiene Foundation supports and practices this solution to germ control. Stephanie will now visualize a future without limited use of antibacterial products.

IV. **Fourth Main Point (Visualization):** Continued abuse of antibacterial products presents a dangerous future for germ control.

Listener Relevance: We've all heard stories on the news about colds and flus developing in new, never before seen strains.

A. **Subpoint:** Strings of resistant bacteria will develop.

1. **Sub-Subpoint:** A Tufts University Health & Nutrition Letter from October 1998 states that overkill can backfire. "It can lead to the development of bacteria that will be able to withstand the action of antibacterial agents should they ever really be needed." (Antibacterial Overkill, 1998)

2. **Sub-Subpoint:** Stuart Levy explains in a *New York Times* article, "Like antibiotics, antibacterials can alter the mix of bacteria; they simultaneously kill susceptible bacteria and promote the growth of resistant strains … and now are available to thrive thanks to the destruction of competing microbes." (Brody, 2000)

  B. **Subpoint:** Bacteria will mutate and we will run out of defenses.

1. **Sub-Subpoint:** "The more they're used, the more the bacteria that they are supposed to destroy will undergo mutations that only serve to strengthen them by allowing them to 'resist' the antibacterial attacks." (Antibacterial Overkill, 1998)

2. **Sub-Subpoint:** As the June 28, 2000, Minneapolis *Star Tribune* describes, "Chemicals can stick around in the home and continue to select for resistance when the levels of these chemicals drop. Then even high levels of the chemicals won't work." (Brody, 2000)

Transition: Stephanie has clearly described the dangerous possibilities of antibacterial product abuse. Luckily, the future for germ control doesn't have to be so bleak.

Conclusion

I. **Action/(Action Step):** YOU can protect yourself from germs without antibacterial products. The solution is simple: Wash Your Hands! Ironically, the America that cleans with antibacterial products shows an astonishing unwillingness to take such a simple step. According to the American Society of Microbiology, a study of 7,836 people in restrooms in Chicago, Atlanta, New York, New Orleans and San Francisco, just 58 percent washed their hands! (Kolata, 2001, p. On-line)

II. **Listener Relevance:** It doesn't matter where you are or what you are doing. If you are getting on the subway, speaking on a public phone, or sitting in your classroom – you can protect yourself from germs without the use of antibacterial products.

III. **Speaker Credibility:** Through our research, we've found that America's obsession with germs can be handled effectively without the use of antibacterial products.

IV. **Thesis Restatement:** We hope we've convinced you that America's overuse of antibacterial products is indeed reducing their effectiveness as germ fighters.

V. **Main Point Summary:** Today, Megan identified the abuse of antibacterial products and described the dangerous consequences, Stephanie proposed a future of continued abuse, and Daniel detailed a simple solution to an increasingly complex problem.

VI. **Clincher:** The next time you're boarding the subway or sitting in class – remember, you can be germ free – without the use of antibacterial products.

194

References

Brody, J. (2000, June 28). 'Antibacterial' may be antihealthy bacteria-killing cleansers and products actually may help create the superbug that many fear, health experts warn. *Star Tribune*, p. 2E.

Brody, J. (2000, June 20). How germ-phobia can lead to illness. *New York Times*, p. 8F.

Burcum, Jill (2000, Dec. 19). Debugging the holidays: Spreading cheer doesn't have to mean spreading germs – or getting them. *Star Tribune*, p.1E.

Davis, Elizabeth, A. (1999, Oct. 24). Despite questions of efficacy, antibacterials clean up; hygiene: sales of germ-killing consumer products are booming, despite warnings that they could lead to super-bugs resistant to antibiotics. *The Los Angeles Times*, p. 9.

Kolata, Gina (2001, Jan. 7). Kill all the bacteria! *New York Times*, p. 4.1.

Leland, John (2000, Aug. 31). Yes, there's such a thing as too clean. *New York Times*, p. F.1.

Leland, John (2000, Sep. 12). Too clean? Studies show it's possible. *Star Tribune*, p. 1E.

Mayer, Caroline E. (1999, Sep. 17). FTC challenges antibacterial product claims. *The Washington Post*, p. A9.

Rosin, Hanna (1999, May 9). Germ warfare. *The Washington Post*, p. W6.

(1998). Antibacterial overkill. *Tufts University Health & Nutrition Letter*, *16*, 1-4.

ACTUATION PERSUASIVE SYMPOSIUM SPEECH EXAMPLE
Individual Member Outline Example

Formal Outline: "Problems with Antibacterial Products"
Megan Gilderhus

Introduction

I. **Attention Catcher:** The November 10th, 1997 edition of *The New Republic* states that half of all Americans go out of their way to buy antibacterial products whenever possible.

II. **Listener Relevance:** As consumers, we should all be concerned about antibacterial overuse.

III. **Speaker Credibility:** Through my research, I've learned that antibacterial products lose their effectiveness when not used in moderation.

IV. **Thesis:** Practical, not obsessive use of antibacterial products is essential for total germ protection.

V. **Preview:** Today, I'll discuss our over-use of antibacterial products. I'll point out the misleading advertising that gives us a false sense of security and finally, I'll warn you of the dangerous consequences of antibacterial product over-use.

Transition: Let's start by looking at the over-use of antibacterial products.

Body

I. **First Main Point:** Americans are overusing antibacterial products.

Listener Relevance: Have you ever noticed how often disk jockeys replay new songs on the radio? After a while, you get tired of hearing the same songs. Similar to this overplay is America's overuse of antibacterial products.

A. **Subpoint:** We are obsessed with being clean and will buy any product that promises complete germ removal.

 1. **Sub-Subpoint:** One in five Americans has a family member who is obsessed with germs. (Rosin, 1997, p. On-line).

 2. **Sub-Subpoint:** 39% of Americans said they have changed their cleaning habits due to germs. (Rosin, 1997, p. On-line.)

B. **Subpoint:** Antibacterial product advertising creates a false sense of security.

C. **Subpoint:** A recent survey conducted for the Infectious Diseases Society of America found that nearly half of all soaps on the market now contain antibacterial agents (Leland, 2000, p. On-line).

Transition: Now that I've discussed some of the problems with antibacterial products, I'll describe the consequences of our over-use.

II. **Second Main Point:** An effect of overusing antibacterial products is reduced effectiveness.

Listener Relevance: None of us like to feel dirty. We take showers or baths, wear cologne and perfume and apply deodorants and powders daily. Unfortunately, this "need to be clean" can be dangerous.

A. **Subpoint:** Overuse of antibacterial products may increase illness and bring on new germs.

   1. **Sub-Subpoint:** There is a growing contention that we don't have enough germs and dirt in our lives.

   2. **Sub-Subpoint:** As Dr. Andrew Liu, pediatric asthma specialist at the National Jewish Medical Research Center in Denver states in the aforementioned *Tribune* article, "We're finding that childhood exposure to infections and certain environmental toxins seems to have a protective effect."

B. **Subpoint:** Bacteria are showing signs of resistance to antibacterial agents.

C. **Subpoint:** Popular antibacterial hand soaps provide protection, but they do not sterilize hands and they are not approved by the FDA. (Davis, 1999, p. On-line).

Conclusion

I. **Thesis restatement:** In conclusion, practical, not obsessive use of antibacterial products is essential for total germ protection.

II. **Main point summary:** Today, we have discussed Americans' overuse of antibacterial products and how this may lower effectiveness of antibacterial products.

III. **Clincher:** As stated in the November 10th 1997 edition of *The New Republic*, half of all Americans buy antibacterial products whenever possible, but with this new information, I hope you think twice about making that purchase.

References

Davis, Elizabeth A. (1999). Despite questions of efficacy, antibacterials clean up. *The Los Angeles Times.*

ACTUATION PERSUASIVE SYMPOSIUM SPEECH EXAMPLE
Individual Member Outline Example

Formal Outline: "Solutions to Germ Removal"
Daniel Grothues

Introduction

I. **Attention Catcher:** How can we help prevent the spread of resistant bacteria?

II. **Listener Relevance:** We all have to be more responsible.

III. **Speaker Credibility:** Through my research I have developed a plan of action that everyone can easily follow.

IV. **Thesis:** There are several alternative solutions to germ removal.

V. **Preview:** Today, we'll examine some alternative solutions to antibacterial products. In particular, the solution can be found through the use of regular soap and by simply being more practical with antibacterial products.

Transition: According to the Minneapolis *Star Tribune*, December 19, 2000, hand washing with regular soap is still the best way to prevent infection.

Body

I. **First Main Point:** Antibacterial products advertising promises more than most products can produce, thus the consumer has to develop an awareness of this fact.

   A. **Subpoint:** According to many scientists and government officials advertising on these products is misleading. Also the Environmental Protection Agency (EPA) has disciplined several companies for exaggerated claims.

   B. **Subpoint:** Hasbro advertised that its antibacterial toys and highchairs "protect your child from germs and bacteria." The EPA made Hasbro change the claim after it was found untrue.

Transition: While increased awareness is a solution for practical germ protection, moderated use of these products is the best alternative.

II. **Second Main Point:** If you do use antibacterial products, use them in moderation.

   A. **Subpoint:** We've gone overboard trying to kill everything in the environment.

   B. **Subpoint:** As a result the Federal Trade Commission (FTC) has begun cracking down on germ-fighting claims being made for a growing number of antibacterial products.

   C. **Subpoint:** Jodie Bernstein, Director of the FTC's Bureau of Consumer Protection says, "the message we hope to send consumers is 'Don't think that these products give you any better protection than washing your hands with soap and hot water.'"

Transition: Not just the moderated use of antibacterial products, but also proper hygiene practices are the focus of our solution.

198

III. **Third Main Point:** For practical germ removal, the solution is simple.

    A. **Subpoint:** Hand-washing. This is the tip mentioned first by everyone. It sounds simple, but it is still the best way to prevent infection.

    B. **Subpoint:** However, doing correctly is important. The U.S. Centers for Disease Control and Prevention recommends this process: Wet hands with warm soap and water, lather up with soap, rub hands together briskly for 10 seconds, rinse, and dry off with a paper towel.

Conclusion

I. **Thesis restatement:** In conclusion, there are several alternative solutions to germ removal.

II. **Main point summary:** Today, we discussed several solutions to germ removal. Be an alert consumer, moderate your use of antibacterial products, and practice proper hygiene habits.

III. **Clincher:** By now you should have an idea of how to be an aware consumer to prevent the spread of resistant bacteria.

References

Mayer, Caroline E. (1999, Sep. 17). FTC challenges antibacterial product claims. *The Washington Post*, p. A9.

Burcum, Jill (2000, Dec. 19). Debugging the holidays: Spreading cheer doesn't have to mean spreading germs – or getting them. *Star Tribune*, p.1E.

ACTUATION PERSUASIVE SPEECH SYMPOSIUM EXAMPLE
Individual Member Outline Example

Formal Outline: "Visualizing the Future"
Stephanie Ahlfeldt

Introduction

I. **Attention Catcher:** It's the bleak winter season again … and every other person seems to be ill and determined to spread his or her germs. The grocery store checker sneezes as she scans the produce. The man on the train coughs constantly as his seatmate scrunches against the window and turns her head away … But there also is a counter-insurgency out there, armed with an arsenal of hand soaps, sprays for the bathroom and kitchen countertops, dishwashing detergents, lotions, Band-Aids, toothbrushes, toothpaste, even chopsticks with chemicals guaranteed to kill household germs. The army is deployed despite scientists' repeated warnings that the more you try to kill germs, the stronger they become. Not only are new studies showing that more and more bacteria are becoming impervious to antibiotics, but there are studies showing that, at least in the laboratory, bacteria can become resistant to the germ-killing chemicals in soaps and cleansers.

II. **Listener Relevance:** This is a scary story for us to hear being we all use antibacterial products, even if it is just to wash our hands after using a public restroom. This *New York Times* article from January 7, 2001 points out important information for us to consider.

III. **Speaker Credibility:** Personally, I use antibacterial products daily and am surprised to find in my research that I may actually be harming myself and others.

IV. **Thesis:** Continued abuse of antibacterial products presents a dangerous future for germ control.

V. **Preview:** Today, we will examine our future with the continued use of antibacterial products. We will discuss the possibilities of resistant bacteria strains developing, and the mutation of bacteria that we will eventually not be able to defend against.

Transition: Let's start by examining the possibility of resistant bacteria developing.

Body

I. **First Main Point:** Strains of resistant bacteria will develop.

A. **Subpoint:** A Tufts University Health and Nutrition Letter from October 1998 states that overkill can backfire. "It can lead to the development of bacteria that will be able to withstand the action of antibacterial agents should they ever be needed."

B. **Subpoint:** Stuart Levy explains in a *New York Times* article "Like antibiotics, antibacterials can alter the mix of bacteria; they simultaneously kill susceptible bacteria and promote the growth of resistant strains . . . and now are available to thrive thanks to the destruction of competing microbes."

Transition: The thought of resistant strains developing is a very serious problem, but what about when bacteria begin to mutate and we run out of resources for our defense?

200

II. **Second Main Point:** Bacteria will mutate, and we will run out of defenses.

    A. **Subpoint:** "The more they're used, the more the bacteria that they are supposed to destroy will undergo mutations that only serve to strengthen them by allowing them to 'resist' the antibacterial attacks" (Antibacterial Overkill, 1998).

    B. **Subpoint:** *The Star Tribune* from June 28, 2001 describes, "Chemicals can stick around in the home and continue to select for resistance when the levels of these chemicals drop. Then even high levels of the chemicals won't work" (Brody, 2000).

    Transition: Now it is easy to see how dangerous the overuse of antbacterial products truly is.

Conclusion

I. **Thesis restatement:** Continued abuse of antibacterial products does, in fact, present a dangerous future for germ control.

II. **Main point summary:** Today, we have examined our future with the continued use of antibacterial products. We discussed the possibilities of resistant bacteria strains developing and the mutation of bacteria that we will not be able to defend against.

III. **Clincher:** The next time you are in public and are exposed to people coughing and sneezing, avoid reaching for your hand sanitizer. It could make next winter's cold even worse!

References

Brody, J. (2000, June 28). " 'Antibacterial' may be anti healthy. Bacteria-killing cleansers and products actually may help create the superbug that many fear, health experts warn." *Star Tribune*, p. 2E.

Brody, J. (2000, June 20). "How germ-phobia can lead to illness." *The New York Times*, p. 8F.

Kolata, G. (2000, January 7). "Kill all the bacteria!" *The New York Times*, p. 4. 1.

Tufts University (1998). "Antibacterial overkill." Tufts University *Health and Nutrition Letter*, 16, 1-4.

ACTUATION PERSUASIVE SYMPOSIUM SPEECH EXAMPLE
Monroe's Motivated Squence Design

Formal Outline: "Cloning"

Pete Cossette, Matt Feist, Desmond Maas, Jaime Sundsbak, and Wendi Gifford

Introduction:

I. **Attention Step:** Science and technology today are like a wild horse, you can get a rope around its neck but no halter or saddle before it takes off running with you dragging behind. Announcements of discoveries and accomplishments are made, and before we can consider, let alone comprehend them, the next is announced.

II. **Listener Relevance Link.** One of science and technology's latest announcements was the birth of Dolly the sheep. Cloning technology brought her to us, and this same technology will be a part of the future for us all.

III. **Speaker Credibility:** Pete, Matt, Desmond, Jaime, and I are here today to discuss the findings of our research on cloning.

IV. **Thesis Statement:** Cloning is a technology that needs restraint. We need to be able to slow it down, examine it thoroughly, and give it guidelines before it is allowed to proceed.

V. **Preview of Speech:** Today, we will examine some of the problems with cloning, the causes of these problems, offer some solutions, and give you a peek into our future with cloning. Pete will share with us the practical and ethical problems of human cloning. Matt will reveal weak legislation, the drive for fame and fortune, and the quest for ultimate power as causes for the concern that cloning presents. Desmond will offer some solutions on the national level, local level, and let you know what you can do personally. Finally, Jaime will take you on a trip into the future where cloning has not been restrained and where it has been given boundaries.

Transition: Now Pete will examine some of the problems that cloning has presented.

Body

I. **First Main Point (Need–Problem):** Cloning presents practical and ethical questions.

A. **Subpoint:** There are practical problems associated with cloning in general.

1. **Sub-Subpoint:** According to The Learning Channel's program *Amazing Discoveries* on cloning, it took 276 unsuccessful attempts before Dolly the sheep was finally born.

2. **Sub-Subpoint:** Sheep cells are more receptive to cloning than human cells. How many human embryos would be destroyed before a viable clone would be made?

B. **Subpoint:** Human cloning has many ethical problems.

1. **Sub-Subpoint:** As Leon Kass put it in his testimony to the National Bioethics Advisor Commission on March 14, 1997, "the cloned person may experience concerns about his distinctive identity not only because he will be identical to another person, but that person might be his father or mother."

2. **Sub-Subpoint:** They will feel pressure to perform up to expectations.

3. **Sub-Subpoint:** Leon Kass also stated in his testimony that when parents choose to procreate, they are saying yes not only to having a child but to having whatever child this turns out to be.

4. **Sub-Subpoint:** According to Leon Kass, if we give up this chance, then our children become our property and possession and that we want to control their future.

Transition: Pete has described some of the problems that cloning has presented to us. Next, let's hear from Matt what causes these problems.

II. **Second Main Point (Need-Cause):** Reckless scientists without restraint are the cause of one of the reasons for concern with cloning.

A. **Subpoint:** Legislation on the matter is extremely scarce.

1. **Sub-Subpoint:** President Clinton is currently working on developing an international ban on cloning.

2. **Sub-Subpoint:** United Nation world leaders are working on it.

B. **Subpoint:** Some people want to clone simply for fame and fortune.

3. **Sub-Subpoint:** Dr. Richard Seed and his profitable "fertility" clinic.

C. **Subpoint:** The quest for ultimate power and playing God.

1. **Sub-Subpoint:** Jerry Shaw, the Washington State Coalition Director, does not like the idea of cloning people just for medical reasons.

2. **Sub-Subpoint:** Immoral to have clones as a piece of property for use by owners.

3. **Sub-Subpoint:** Rabbi Elliot Dorf, professor of philosophy at the university of Bel Air California, speaks of how we might possibly clone.

4. **Sub-Subpoint:** Those that should not be cloned and what might happen if they were.

Transition: Now that some of the problems and their causes concerning cloning are fresh in our minds, Desmond will propose some solutions.

III. **Third Main Point (Satisfaction–Solution):** Our solution has three steps: The International and National legislation, education, and individual votes.

A. **Subpoint:** International and National laws will have to be made, followed, and enforced.

1. **Sub-Subpoint:** According to the American Bioethics Commission: "Federal legislation must be enacted to prohibit anyone from attempting, whether in research or a clinical setting, to create a child somatic cell nuclear transfer for cloning. It is critical, however, that such legislation include a sunset clause to ensure Congress will review the issue after a specified period of time."

2. **Sub-Subpoint:** Ban to take effect immediately on international as well as national levels.

3. **Sub-Subpoint:** The penalties for violating must be stiff enough to deter the scientific community from attempting this unethical act.

4. **Sub-Subpoint:** Penalties to include maximum of 5 years of incarceration.

B. **Subpoint:** A solution to cloning on a local level.

1. **Sub-Subpoint:** According to Dr. Donald Bruce of the Church of Scotland: "Society as a whole must own research which is normally being done on its behalf. This can happen

only if there is true participation. Encouragement needs to be given to the ethical training of scientists themselves."

    2. **Sub-Subpoint:** We need to be educated in the ethical and moral side of this issue.

    3. **Sub-Subpoint:** Enrollment in an ethics course at a university or community education facility being made heard.

  C. **Subpoint:** We as individuals can become involved in the decisions.

    1. **Sub-Subpoint:** Contact your Congress person or Senator to make your concerns.

    2. **Sub-Subpoint:** Attend panel discussions in your area.

    3. **Sub-Subpoint:** Find out where your representatives stand on the issue and make your voice heard through the voting process.

Transition: Thank you Desmond for offering some solutions to this problem. Now we will hear from Jaime. He will give us a glimpse into our future with cloning.

IV. **Fourth Main Point (Visualization):** If we don't let our moral and ethical thoughts catch up with our scientific thoughts, the consequences will be disastrous.

  A. **Subpoint:** "Bad" world in which cloning is unregulated.

    1. **Sub-Subpoint:** Trying to be something that you are not.

    2. **Sub-Subpoint:** Doors warming up for Mozart.

    3. **Sub-Subpoint:** *Multiplicity*, Michael Keaton portrays a man who has no time. (*Multiplicity*, 1996).

    4. **Sub-Subpoint:** The outcome would be overpopulation.

    5. **Sub-Subpoint:** Cloning takes over as primary form of reproduction.

    6. **Sub-Subpoint:** With a drop of blood, doctors know time and cause of your death. (*GAATACA*, 1997).

  B. **Subpoint:** "Good" world where cloning is regulated.

    1. **Sub-Subpoint:** Regeneration will create new limbs and organs for us. (Dixon, 1994).

    2. **Sub-Subpoint:** Disease fighting "Supergenes" inserted at birth to fight off disease. (Dixon, 1994).

    3. **Sub-Subpoint:** Useful medicines created in cloned animals. (Dixon, 1994).

Transition: We have discussed the problems that cloning presents and their causes. Now we must put into motion some of the valuable steps that have been proposed to ensure an acceptable future with cloning.

Conclusion

I. **Thesis restatement:** We need to slow cloning technology down. We need time to ask our questions and find answers. We need to take the steps to create boundaries for this technology in order to insure our future with cloning is a good one.

II. **Main point summary:** We have introduced the problems that cloning has presented, some of the causes of these problems, some solutions, and looked at our future with cloning being involved.

III. **Clincher:** Remember the best way to tame a wild horse is to first lead it into a coral. With patience, knowledge, and experience you will be able to slip that halter over his head, apply a saddle, and ride off over the hills.

References

Poll: Most Americans say cloning is wrong (http://cnn.com)

Amazing Discoveries. (1998) Cloning (television), The Learning Channel

Kass, Leon R. Cloning of human beings (www.all.org) (1998)

Executive summary of the American Bioethics Commission, (1997) [online]
http:// bioethics.gov/cgi.bin/biorth-counter pl

Donald Bruce, Director, Ph.D. (1997) General Assembly Report on Cloning Animals and Humans, Society, Religion and Technology Project, Logo Church of Scotland [online]
http://webzone/co.uk/www/srtproject/ga97clon.htm

GAATACA, Columbia Tri-Star, 1997.

Multiplicity, Columbia Tri-Star, 1996.

Dixon, Patrick. *The genetic revolution.* Westly Owen Books, London, England, 1994, pp. 12–15.

Mohammed, Arshad. Clinton proposes 5-year ban on human cloning. [online]
http:/www.prolife.org/ultimate/un22.html

Yahoo. Democrats seek 10-year ban on human cloning. [online]
http://www.yahoo.com/headlines/980203/politics/stories/cloning_l.html

ACTUATION PERSUASIVE SYMPOSIUM SPEECH EXAMPLE
Individual Member Outline Example

Formal Outline: "Problems Associated with Cloning"
Pete Cossette

Introduction

I. **Attention Catcher:** Imagine, for a moment, if you were walking down the street and ran into someone who looked exactly like you. No big deal, right? Lots of people have identical twins. Take that one step further though . . . this other person is made up of the same cells and has the same DNA in the same configurations as you do. Scary? We think so!

II. **Listener Relevance:** Since all of us are living through huge advances in technology and science, it is difficult for us to even imagine what is possible through science. However, because the push for advances continues, we will all be affected in some way or another by what scientists all over the world are testing and discovering.

III. **Speaker Credibility:** I was interested in the subject of cloning ever since the story about Dolly the Sheep hit the news. Since then, I have spent much time thinking about the consequences of cloning and doing research to educate myself further about this scientific breakthrough.

IV. **Thesis Statement:** There are many problems associated with the notion of cloning.

V. **Preview of Main Points:** Today, let's examine how both the practical and the ethical concerns of cloning far outweigh any potential benefits that could come from the practice of cloning.

Transition: Let's start by examining the practical problems associated with human cloning.

Body

I. **First Main Point:** Cloning presents practical problems.

   A. **Subpoint:** According to the Learning Channel's program *Amazing Discoveries*, it took 276 unsuccessful attempts before Dolly the sheep was finally born.

   B. **Subpoint:** Sheep cells are more receptive to cloning than human cells. How many human embryos would be destroyed before a viable clone would be made?

   C. **Subpoint:** How much would this process cost?

Transition: While cloning presents many practical concerns, the problem of cloning doesn't end there. There are also many ethical concerns involved with cloning humans.

II. **Second Main Point:** Human cloning has many ethical problems as well.

   A. **Subpoint:** As Leon Kass put it in his testimony to the National Bioethics Advisor Commission on March 14, 1997, "The cloned person may experience concerns about his distinctive identity, not only because he will be identical to another person, but because that person might be his own father or mother."

      1. **Sub-Subpoint:** They will feel pressure to perform up to expectations.

B. **Subpoint:** Leon Kass also states in his testimony that when parents choose to procreate, they are saying yes not only to accepting children, but to accepting whatever the child turns out to be.

    1. **Sub-Subpoint:** According to Kass, if we give up this chance, our children become our property and possession, and we want to control their future.

Conclusion

I. **Thesis restatement:** In conclusion, there are many problems associated with the notion of cloning.

II. **Main point summary:** Today, we have covered both the practical and the ethical concerns regarding human cloning.

III. **Clincher:** Imagine, for a moment, if you were walking down the street and ran into someone who looked exactly like you. No big deal—right? Lots of people have identical twins. Take that one step further though . . . this other person not only looks like you, but also thinks like you and is made up of the same DNA as you. Now you tell me if you think that would pose a problem for you or not!

References

Executive summary of the American Bioethics Commission, (1997) [online] http://bioethics.gov/cgi.bin/biorth-counter

Kass, L. R. (1998). Cloning of human beings. (www.all.org)

Amazing Discoveries. (1998) Cloning (television), The Learning Channel.

ACTUATION PERSUASIVE SYMPOSIUM SPEECH EXAMPLE
Individual Member Outline Example

Formal Outline: "Causes of the Rapid Interest and Action of Cloning"
Matt Feist

Introduction

I. **Attention Catcher:** If you had the power to play God, would you?

II. **Listener Relevance:** Because cloning has received so much attention lately, it is something we are all aware of and something that has the potential to touch us all in some way or another.

III. **Speaker Credibility:** I have often wondered why people would want to clone human beings, and through research I have found that answer.

IV. **Thesis Statement:** Today, let's look more closely at what causes people to become involved in the cloning process.

V. **Preview of Main Points:** Specifically, we'll examine the lack of legislation concerning the matter, the fame and fortune many scientists are seeking through cloning, and the feeling of ultimate power or "playing God" that is associated with cloning.

Transition: Because cloning is a relatively new phenomenon, there is little law or legislation concerning it.

Body

I. **First Main Point:** Legislation on the matter is extremely scarce.

  A. **Subpoint:** According to the web page "Clinton proposes a 5-year ban on human cloning" by Arshad Mohammed, President Clinton is currently working on developing a ban on international cloning.

  B. **Subpoint:** United Nation world leaders are also working on implementing guidelines to control the growth of interest in cloning in the scientific communities of the world.

Transition: Because the leaders of the world are still working toward banning cloning, some scientists are engaged in the process for the fame and fortune that are associated with such a scientific milestone.

II. **Second Main Point:** Some people want to clone simply for the fame and fortune.

  A. **Subpoint:** Dr. Richard Seed and his profitable "fertility" clinic (Website Democrats seek 10-year ban on human cloning).

  B. **Subpoint:** Fame comes with cloning.

    1. **Sub-Subpoint:** Scientist who cloned Dolly became famous overnight.

    2. **Sub-Subpoint:** Television appearances, book deals, and speaking opportunities all bring in money for those involved in the cloning process.

Transition: For some, it isn't just the fame and fortune associated with cloning that draws them into doing it, but instead it is the ultimate form of playing God.

II. **Third Main Point:** There is a quest for the ultimate power of playing God.

    A. **Subpoint:** Jerry Shaw, the Washington State Coalition Director, does not like the idea of cloning people just for medical reasons.

        1. **Sub-Subpoint:** Scientists trying to provide a "quick fix."

        2. **Sub-Subpoint:** Consequences to playing God are huge.

    B. **Subpoint:** Immoral to have clones as pieces of property for use by owners and scientists to do with what they like.

    C. **Subpoint:** According to Dixon in his book, *The Genetic Revolution*, Rabbi Elliot Dorf, professor of Philosophy at the University of Bel Air California, speaks of how we might choose possible clones.

        1. **Sub-Subpoint:** What if scientists clone "bad" people? Double the problem.

        2. **Sub-Subpoint:** Unnatural increase in population = decline in food, resources, etc., for the rest of the population.

Conclusion

I. **Thesis restatement:** So today, we've examined what the causes of the cloning craze are.

II. **Main point summary:** Specifically, we've revealed the lack of legislation concerning the matter, the fame and fortune many scientists are seeking through cloning, and the feeling of ultimate power or "playing God" that is associated with cloning.

III. **Clincher:** So if you had the power to play God knowing what you now know, what would you say? Is it worth it?

References

Dixon, P. (1994). *The genetic revolution*. Westly Owen Books, London, pp. 12–15.

Mohammed, Arshad. Clinton proposes 5-year ban on human cloning. [online]
http://www.prolife.org/ultimate/un22.html

Yahoo. Democrats seek 10-year ban on human cloning. [online]
www.yahoo.com/headlines/980203/politics/stories/cloning_1.html

ACTUATION PERSUASIVE SYMPOSIUM SPEECH EXAMPLE
Individual Member Outline Example

Formal Outline: "Solutions to the Current Problems Associated with Cloning"

Desmond Maas

Introduction

I. **Attention Catcher:** The faster science and technology proceed, the more difficult it becomes to regulate the sensitive issues that arise from these questionable advances.

II. **Listener Relevance:** We have all heard some discussion on the possibility of human cloning, and, although it seems as though the solution to the moral and ethical concerns seems very clear, it is obviously a very complex subject.

III. **Speaker Credibility:** I have looked at the current legislation in some depth and have seen many of the proposals to solve the ethical battle of human cloning.

IV. **Thesis Statement:** Current legislation must be reformed immediately, and more specific solutions must be implemented for the future.

V. **Preview of Speech:** Today, I will propose to you new national legislation on human cloning that will be much more effective in controlling the ethical and moral progress. I will then show you the solutions on a local level to enhance education to the current issues as well as the issues to come. Finally I will tell you what we all need to do as individuals to ensure these changes are made.

Body

I. **First Main Point:** Solution to cloning on a national level.

A. **Subpoint:** Obviously human cloning for the mere sake of satisfying our curiosity should be banned worldwide. There should be no need for the experimentation of human subjects or embryos until the procedures have become practical and safe. In no way should all possible advances be prohibited, but there needs to be an ethical boundary of what can advance and what should be held off limits until the benefits are safe and practical. We propose a total ban on all human clone research until it can be done safely and has some practical use. *According to the American Bioethics Commission "Federal legislation must be enacted to prohibit anyone from attempting, whether in research, or a clinical setting, to create a child somatic cell nuclear transfer for cloning. It is critical however, that such legislation include a sunset clause to ensure congress will review the issue after a specified period of time."*

1. **Sub-Subpoint:** This ban will take effect immediately and must be implemented on the international as well as the national level. Any clone reproduction of a human child is to be prohibited. Research will continue on safe and practical applications; however, this research must be restricted by clear language that eliminates confusion on what is appropriate.

2. **Sub-Subpoint:** The penalties for violating must be stiff enough to deter the scientific community from attempting this unethical act. We propose a penalty of one million dollars to any individual that attempts to violate this legislation. And a fine of ten million to

any firm, clinic, hospital, laboratory, or research facility engaged in illegal cloning activity. Also, the individual will permanently lose all professional licenses to prevent any future research by the individual.

3. **Sub-Subpoint:** The penalties also must include incarceration—we propose a prison sentence of not more than 5 years to deter the unethical from attempting to perform unauthorized acts of Human cloning.

Transition: Now that I have told you of the solution that we must implement on a national and international level, I will now show you what must be done on a local level.

II. **Second Main Point:** Solution to cloning on a local level.

  A. **Subpoint:** The possible solutions to end the controversy of human cloning begin with society becoming educated and informed of the issues involved.

    1. **Sub-Subpoint:** *According to Dr. Donald Bruce of the Church of Scotland: "Society as a whole must own research which is normally being done on its behalf. This can happen only if there is true participation. Encouragement needs to be given to the ethical training of scientists themselves."*

  B. **Subpoint:** Education is the key to eliminating this dilemma between what is ethical and moral.

    1. **Sub-Subpoint:** We need to be educated in the ethical and moral side of this issue. Colleges and universities across the country need to intertwine this topic in all ethics courses, especially science, engineering, and medical courses.

  C. **Subpoint:** We need to make our voices heard of the concern we feel about what the scientific community is doing.

    1. **Sub-Subpoint:** A first step is to enroll in an ethics course at the university or wherever one is available—this does not apply to certain professions; this applies to all disciplines.

Transition: Now that we have shown you the solution on a local level, let us now see what needs to be done on a personal level.

I. **Solution on a Personal Level.**

  A. **Subpoint:** Another action that will ensure an ethical future is for all of us to become involved in the decisions being made.

    1. **Sub-Subpoint:** In order to be involved in the decisions that affect us, we need to become active participants. Contact your Congress person or Senator to make your concerns heard.

    2. **Sub-Subpoint:** Make your voice heard through the voting process, find out where your representatives stand on the issues.

    3. **Sub-Subpoint:** Attend panel discussions in your area to familiarize yourself with the issues.

Conclusion

I. **Thesis restatement:** Current legislation must be modified and improved to incorporate a more distinct separation between what is acceptable and what is not, so that solutions to controversial issues are more clearly defined.

II. **Main point summary:** Today I told you what must be done to change the current legislation regarding human cloning, I told you what we must do on a local level to educate ourselves and our children on ethical issues, and finally I told you what we all must do to ensure our elected officials express the same concerns we have on these issues.

III. **Clincher:** As science continues to progress, our regulation and control of the sensitive issues produced by new technology must not fall behind.

References

Executive summary of the American Bioethics Commission, (1997) [online] http://bioethics.gov/cgi.bin/biorth_counter.pL

Donald Bruce, Director, PHD. (1997) General Assembly report on cloning animals and humans, society, religion and technology project, Logo Church of Scotland [online] http://webzone/.co.uk/www/srtproject/ga97clon.htm

ACTUATION PERSUASIVE SYMPOSIUM SPEECH EXAMPLE
Individual Member Outline Example

Formal Outline: "Visualization of a World Where Cloning Occurs"
Jaime Sundsbak

Introduction

I. **Attention Catcher:** You walk into a vacant, dark room. You have two options. The first is to turn on the lights and navigate the room successfully. The other option is to flail about in the dark, bumping into things and injuring yourself. Letting cloning progress with the lights off will lead to a very bumpy world.

II. **Listener Relevance Link:** Cloning is going to impact your life and the lives of your children sooner than you think.

III. **Speaker Credibility:** I have read and have watched many versions of our cloning future as envisioned by many different authors.

IV. **Thesis Statement:** If we don't let our moral and ethical thought catch up with our scientific thought, the consequences will be disastrous.

V. **Preview of Speech:** Today, we will look at two versions of our cloning future. What if we don't take measures to understand and legislate cloning? We will envision this world through a mixture of Hollywood imagery. With proper legislation and education, cloning can be a benefit to society. We will examine this wonderful world by examining a world where cloning technology is controlled, but utilized.

Transition: So let's jump into our first world, a world where laws and governments have not kept up with science.

Body

I. **First Main Point:** "Bad" world in which cloning is a part.

  A. **Subpoint:** Cloning museums.

    1. **Sub-Subpoint:** Trying to be something that you are not.

    2. **Sub-Subpoint:** Doors warming up for Mozart.

  B. **Subpoint:** Clone to save time

    1. **Sub-Subpoint:** *Multiplicity*, Michael Keaton portrays a man who has no time (*Multiplicity*, 1996).

    2. **Sub-Subpoint:** This would lead to overpopulation.

  C. **Subpoint:** Mating practices

    1. **Sub-Subpoint:** Cloning has taken over as primary form of reproduction.

    2. **Sub-Subpoint:** With a drop of blood, doctors know time and cause of your death (*GAATACA*, 1997).

Transition: This would lead to a dark sterile, controlled world we all would live in. Let's now examine a world where cloning would be legislated and used only in certain humane circumstances.

II. **Second Main Point:** "Good" world where cloning is a part.

    A. **Subpoint:** Concepts judged "good" by society will be implemented.

        1. **Sub-Subpoint:** Regeneration will create new limbs and organs for us (Dixon, 1994).

        2. **Sub-Subpoint:** Disease fighting "Supergenes" inserted at birth to fight off disease (Dixon, 1994).

        3. **Sub-Subpoint:** Useful medicines created in cloned animals (Dixon, 1994).

Transition: We can see this world will have the promise of a bright future for our children and ourselves.

Conclusion

I. **Thesis restatement:** Through the examples just presented, we can see that the moral use of cloning will benefit our society as much as the immoral use of it could destroy our community.

II. **Main point summary:** We have seen a world where there are no "checks" on cloning and found it to be one of triviality, frivolity, and domination over the human spirit. This is a world where cloning is controlled, but the benefits of the technology are there. They can give us a new chance at life, eliminate disease, and help provide us with vital life fluids that will sustain us.

III. **Clincher:** So when we enter that darkened room of cloning together, let's all have the strength to shine the light of truth so we can enter into a new area for mankind.

References

GAATACA, Columbia Tri-Star, 1997.

Multiplicity, Columbia Tri-Star, 1996.

Dixon, Patrick. *The Genetic Revolution*. Westly Owen Books, London, England, 1994, pp. 12–15.

ACTUATION PERSUASIVE SYMPOSIUM SPEECH EXAMPLE
Problem–Cause–Solution Design

Formal Outline: "Solving the Problem of Gang Violence in America"
Matt Coumbe, Shannon Vanhorn, Pamela Zaug and Michelle Snider

Introduction

I. **Attention Step:** Forty years ago, a gang meant a group of friends who would play ball, roller skate, and hang out at the ice cream shop. Today, a gang is a group of friends who play games, but these games that leave young people dead and innocent bystanders harmed for no apparent reason.

II. **Listener Relevance Link:** At first, gangs appeared in Los Angeles and New York. Soon, the problem crept to Minneapolis, *Minneapolis/St. Paul Magazine*, June 1992 (story). "Now it's even in Fargo with the death of Cherryl Tendelyn."

III. **Speaker Credibility:** Shannon, Pam, Michelle, and I are here to discuss our research on gangs.

IV. **Thesis Statement:** Gangs are clearly a problem, but not one isolated to a group, culture or community.

V. **Preview:** Today, we will examine not only the problems related to gangs, but also the causes and some solutions. Shannon will talk about gang violence at the national, regional and local level. Pam will talk about why gangs form, what causes the violent actions, and the effects on society. Finally, Michelle will propose a weapon policy, family intervention, and employment options as potential solutions.

Transition: Shannon . . .

Body

I. **First Main Point (Problem):** Gang activity is a problem nationally, regionally, and locally.

A. **Subpoint:** Gang members have increasingly committed crimes and used violence on the national level.

  1. **Sub-Subpoint:** Gangs head 100 drug networks, *Time*, February 2 7, 1995. (Statistics)

  2. **Sub-Subpoint:** Male gang members commit six times more crime than non-gang members from the same socio-economic backgrounds, *Parks and Recreation*, March 1995. (Statistic)

  3. **Sub-Subpoint:** Gang members convene only to fight and cause various types of trouble, *FBI Law Enforcement Bulletin*, January, 1995. (Research Data)

  4. **Sub-Subpoint:** Fifty percent of people killed from gang violence do not belong to gangs, *The Forum*, March 27, 1994. (Statistic)

B. **Subpoint:** Gangs can be found in regional cities.

  1. **Sub-Subpoint:** Gangs can be found in Minneapolis, Minot, Bismarck, and Winnipeg.

  2. **Sub-Subpoint:** Six Grand Forks Air Base men encountered 20 gang members in Winnipeg, *Macleans*, August, 1995. (Example)

C. **Subpoint:** Gangs are prevalent in the Fargo–Moorhead area.

    1. **Sub-Subpoint:** Villa Lobos, ages 8-13, responsible for large number of area crimes, *The Forum*, March 27,1994. (Quote)

    2. **Sub-Subpoint:** Police identify six strong local gangs, *The Forum*, July 16, 1995. (Quote)

    3. **Sub-Subpoint:** Gang member says the crimes will become ruthless, *The Forum*, July 16, 1995. (Quote)

Transition: We heard Shannon describe the problems. Now we need to look at some of the reasons behind this activity.

II. **Second Main Point/Cause:** In recognizing this great problem, it is important for us to understand what is causing this phenomenon.

A. **Subpoint:** There are two reasons why youths join gangs: dysfunctional families and lack of activities.

    1. **Sub-Subpoint:** Dysfunctional families are the main cause of adolescents joining gangs, *USA Today*, January 1994. (Quote)

    2. **Sub-Subpoint:** Many gang members come from impoverished households with absent fathers or fathers who are cold and physically punish them on a regular basis, *USA Today*, January 1994. (Quote)

    3. **Sub-Subpoint:** James C. Howell discusses the impact of lack of activities on adolescents in their choice to join a gang, *Crime and Delinquency*, October, 1994. (Research Data)

B. **Subpoint:** There are two reasons why gang members commit violent acts: gun availability and a shift in attitude.

    1. **Sub-Subpoint:** Each day 100,000 school children carry guns to school, *USA Today*, January 1994. (Quote)

    2. **Sub-Subpoint:** Juvenile arrest rates for weapons-law violations increased 103% between 1985 and 1994, *US News and World Report*, March 1996. (Statistic)

    3. **Sub-Subpoint:** Juvenile killings with firearms quadrupled between 1984 and 1994. Juvenile murderers now use guns in eight out of ten cases, *US World and News Report*, March 1996. (Statistic)

    4. **Sub-Subpoint:** Fox and Pierce state that we have a new generation of youngsters who are inclined to resort to violence over trivial issues, *USA Today*, January, 1994. (Quote)

    5. **Sub-Subpoint:** An example of this is given to us by Kathleen Heide, a Florida psychotherapist and criminologist, *US News and World Report*, March, 1996. (Example)

Transition: We have now looked at this issue in depth at the problems and causes of gang violence. We must now work as a society to carve out solutions. Michelle will propose possible solutions such as weapons policy, family intervention and employment options.

III. **Third Main Point/Solution:** Our solutions will take a three-step approach: parental accountability, reduction of gun availability and positive alternatives.

A. **Subpoint:** The first step is parents and guardians must be held accountable for the actions of their children.

1. **Sub-Subpoint:** President Clinton agrees parental accountability should be enforced, *Press Release: Address to the International Association of Chiefs of Police, October 1994.* (Quote)

2. **Sub-Subpoint:** Florida can charge adults with a felony if they fail to keep loaded guns away from children who shoot someone, *Fortune*, August 1992. (Example)

B. **Subpoint:** The second step is getting guns out of the hands of gang members.

1. **Sub-Subpoint:** Underage children can obtain guns through the illegal gun market, *Newsweek*, August 1993. (Example)

2. **Sub-Subpoint:** An experimental program in Missouri has reduced crime by controlling illegal guns. (Example)

C. **Subpoint:** The third step is providing kids of today with positive alternatives to gang activity.

1. **Sub-Subpoint:** School and community programs must be implemented, *USA Today*, January 1994. (Example)

2. **Sub-Subpoint:** Preventative programs must begin with younger children, *Newsweek*, August 1993. (Example)

Transition: We have now looked at this issue in-depth. We've noted some of the problems and causes of gangs. We must now work as a society to carve out a solution for the future.

Conclusion

I. **Thesis restatement:** We have seen how gangs are a problem not isolated to a group, culture or particular community.

II. **Main point summary:** We've noted some problems and how they've moved from the national to the regional and local level. We have heard why people get involved with gangs and the reason behind the violence. Finally, we have introduced some feasible solutions.

III. **Clincher:** If we join together, we can make our country, cities and neighborhoods safer places to live.

References

Bergman, B. (1995). Wild in the streets: Teenage gangs wreak havoc in Winnipeg. *Macleans*, 108, pp. 18–20.

Bonofonte, J. (1995). Entrepreneurs of crack: An LA street gang transforms itself into a cross-country cocaine empire—until the FBI busts it all over. *Time*, 145, pp. 22–24.

Black youths tell how gangs and guns have them planning their own funerals (1994). *Jet 85*, pp. 26–29.

Davis, R. H. (1995): *FBI law enforcement bulletin*, 64, pp. 16–23.

Eisenman, R. (January 1994). Society confronts the hard-core youthful offender. *USA Today*, pp. 27–28.

Five arrested in California faces charges in Brooklyn (1995). *New York Times*, 145, pp. A 15.

Fox, J. A. and Pierce, G. (January 1994) American killers are getting younger. *USA Today*, pp. 24–26.

Gest, T. and Pope, V. (March 25,1996). Crime time bomb. *US News & World Report*, pp. 28–36.

Gergen, D. (March 25, 1996). Taming teenage wolf packs. *US News & World Report*, pp. 68.

Henkoff, R. (August 10, 1992). Kids are killing, dying, bleeding. *Fortune*, pp. 62–68.

Howell, J. C. (October 1994). Recent gang research: Program and policy implications. *Crime and Delinquency*, pp. 495–515.

Kantrowitz, B. (August 2, 1993). Wild thing in the streets. *Newsweek*, pp. 40–46.

Noble, K. R. (1995). Child is slain, and a neighborhood voices its frustrations. *New York Times*, 145-AT

Press Release: Remarks by the President of the United States to the International Association of Chiefs of Police. October 17,1994. Available from the Office of the Press Secretary, Albuquerque, New Mexico.

Robson, B. (June 1992). Lost boys. *Minneapolis–St. Paul Magazine*, pp. 91–95.

Rodriguez, L. J. (November 21, 1994). Throwaway kids: Turning youth gangs around. *The Nation*, pp. 605–607.

Name _____ Section _____

Title of Speech _____

MEMBER PREPARATION OUTLINE
THE ACTUATION PERSUASIVE SYMPOSIUM SPEECH

Introduction

I. **Attention Catcher:**

II. **Listener Relevance:**

III. **Speaker Credibility:**

IV. **Thesis Statement:**

V. **Preview:**

Body

I. **First Main Point:**

    A. Subpoint:

    B. Supporting Material

    Transition:

II. **Second Main Point:**

    A. Subpoint:

    B. Subpoint:

Conclusion

I. **Thesis restatement:**

II. **Main point summary:**

III. **Clincher:**

Name _____ Section _____

Title of Speech _____

GROUP PREPARATION OUTLINE
THE ACTUATION PERSUASIVE SYMPOSIUM SPEECH

<u>Introduction</u>

I.   **Attention Step:**

II. **Listener Relevance Link:**

III. **Speaker Credibility:**

IV. **Thesis Statement:**

V.   **Preview:**

<u>Body</u>

I.   **First Main Point:**

   A. Subpoint:

      1. Sub-Subpoint:

      2. Sub-Subpoint:

   B. Subpoint:

      1. Sub-Subpoint:

      2. Sub-Subpoint:

   Transition:

II. **Second Main Point:**

   A. Subpoint:

      1. Sub-Subpoint:

      2. Sub-Subpoint:

   B. Subpoint:

      1. Sub-Subpoint:

      2. Sub-Subpoint:

Transition:

III. **Third Main Point:**

    A. Subpoint:

        1. Sub-Subpoint:

        2. Sub-Subpoint:

    B. Subpoint:

        1. Sub-Subpoint:

        2. Sub-Subpoint:

Transition:

Conclusion

I.   **Thesis restatement:**

II. **Main point summary:**

III. **Clincher:**

References

List the references you used in the speech. Format them according to APA style (see Chapter 7 in your textbook for examples).

Name: _____ Section: _____

Title of Speech: _____

INSTRUCTOR CRITIQUE FORM
THE ACTUATION PERSUASIVE SYMPOSIUM SPEECH

Rating Scale   7   6   5   4   3   2   1
             (Excellent)   (Poor)

Individual Grade	**Critique**	**Points**
Delivery		
Use of Voice: Intelligibility? Conversational style? Fluency? Emotional expression?		
Use of Body: Attire? Poise? Eye contact? Facial Expression? Gestures? Use of lectern?		
Structure		
Macrostructure and *Microstructure*		
Content		
Analysis and *Supporting Material* (including PowerPoint visual aid):		

Group Grade	**Critique**	**Points**
Dynamics		
Teamwork? Cooperation? Synergy? (Based on Group Dynamics Peer Critique Forms)		
Content		
Thematic? Substance? Listener relevance? Focus? Supporting Material? Learning styles?		
PowerPoint		
Construction? Integration? Thematic?		

Total Points: _____

THE GROUP SPEECH POLICIES AND PROCEDURES

The Process

1. During the first meeting, groups must develop a "Contract" stating expectations and responsibilities for membership.

2. Members must date and document efforts of other members *each day that the group meets.*

3. At minimum, groups will meet *in the classroom* on each "group work day." At minimum, the instructor *will be present for* the first 15 minutes of those sessions.

4. If a group determines that a particular member is not meeting their responsibilities, the "firing" process can be initiated.

"Firing" a Member

1. Once a group has determined that one member is not meeting their responsibilities, the group meets with that member *(while the instructor is present)* to discuss concerns and agree upon one more chance to live up to expectations. The group, the individual member, and the instructor review and discuss documentation of failed expectations.

2. If the member fails to meet expectations again after the initial meeting (#1), the group has grounds to "fire" them.

3. "Firing" must occur *before* the in-class rehearsal day.

4. A "fired" member must then create and deliver an individual actuation persuasive speech for a maximum of 28 points. (Loss of 21 "group participation" points).

5. All students must turn in "group participation" documentation forms on their scheduled speaking day.

Grievance Procedure: Dissatisfied students may elect to follow the grievance procedure as stated on the syllabus.

REFLECTIVE THINKING PROCESS PAPER GUIDELINES
(5 points each)

Goal: To assess group progress.

Rationale: These papers will help you think critically about the group's progress, as well as about the other member's efforts and your own efforts toward solving a problem and preparing the group speech.

Directions: Prepare a 1- to 2-page typed reflection paper after each group work session. Each paper should focus on three areas:

1. What did the group accomplish in terms of task needs? (Relate this to the process of systematic problem solving or group presentation preparation as detailed in Chapter 18 of the text).

2. Critique the degree to which other members met their ethical responsibilities. (Identify both strengths and suggestions for improvement.)

3. Critique the degree to which you met the ethical responsibilities of group membership. (Identify both your strengths and suggestions for improvement).

Member _____ Critic _____
            (One group member)   (Your name)

GROUP DYNAMICS SUMMATIVE PEER CRITIQUE FORM

Directions: Rate each of your group members using the rating scale:

7	6	5	4	3	2	1
(Excellent)						(Poor)

1) Group Member: _____ Rating: _____
   Comments:

2) Group Member: _____ Rating: _____
   Comments:

3) Group Member: _____ Rating: _____
   Comments:

4) Group Member: _____ Rating: _____
   Comments:

5) Group Member: _____ Rating: _____
   Comments:

Overall Comments:

Member _____ Critic _____
(One group member)   (Your name)

GROUP DYNAMICS PEER CRITIQUE FORM

Directions: Keep written documentation of the ethical group membership of each member in your group using the rating scale:

7	6	5	4	3	2	1
(Excellent)						(Poor)

(1) _____ **Committed to the goals of the group.**
(Rating)

Meeting Date: _____	Meeting Date:_____	Meeting Date:_____
Critique:	Critique:	Critique:

(2) _____ **Fulfills individual assignments.**
(Rating)

Meeting Date:_____	Meeting Date:_____	Meeting Date:_____
Critique:	Critique:	Critique:

228

(3) _____ **Avoids interpersonal conflicts.**
　(Rating)

Meeting Date:_____ Critique:	Meeting Date:_____ Critique:	Meeting Date:_____ Critique:

(4) _____**Encourages group participation.**
　(Rating)

Meeting Date:_____ Critique:	Meeting Date:_____ Critique:	Meeting Date:_____ Critique:

(5) _____ **Helps keep the discussion on track.**
　(Rating)

Meeting Date:_____ Critique:	Meeting Date:_____ Critique:	Meeting Date:_____ Critique:

Member _____ Critic _____
              (One group member)   (Your name)

GROUP DYNAMICS PEER CRITIQUE FORM

Directions: Keep written documentation of the ethical group membership of each member in your group using the rating scale:

7	6	5	4	3	2	1
(Excellent)						(Poor)

(1) _____   **Committed to the goals of the group.**
     (Rating)

Meeting Date: _____	Meeting Date:_____	Meeting Date:_____
Critique:	Critique:	Critique:

(2) _____   **Fulfills individual assignments.**
     (Rating)

Meeting Date:_____	Meeting Date:_____	Meeting Date:_____
Critique:	Critique:	Critique:

(3) _____ **Avoids interpersonal conflicts.**
   (Rating)

Meeting Date:_____ Critique:	Meeting Date:_____ Critique:	Meeting Date:_____ Critique:

(4) _____**Encourages group participation.**
   (Rating)

Meeting Date:_____ Critique:	Meeting Date:_____ Critique:	Meeting Date:_____ Critique:

(5) _____ **Helps keep the discussion on track.**
   (Rating)

Meeting Date:_____ Critique:	Meeting Date:_____ Critique:	Meeting Date:_____ Critique:

Member _____ Critic _____
           (One group member)   (Your name)

GROUP DYNAMICS PEER CRITIQUE FORM

Directions: Keep written documentation of the ethical group membership of each member in your group using the rating scale:

7	6	5	4	3	2	1
(Excellent)						(Poor)

(1) _____ **Committed to the goals of the group.**
    (Rating)

Meeting Date: _____ Critique:	Meeting Date: _____ Critique:	Meeting Date: _____ Critique:

(2) _____ **Fulfills individual assignments.**
    (Rating)

Meeting Date: _____ Critique:	Meeting Date: _____ Critique:	Meeting Date: _____ Critique:

(3) _____ **Avoids interpersonal conflicts.**
    (Rating)

Meeting Date:_____ Critique:	Meeting Date:_____ Critique:	Meeting Date:_____ Critique:

(4) _____**Encourages group participation.**
    (Rating)

Meeting Date:_____ Critique:	Meeting Date:_____ Critique:	Meeting Date:_____ Critique:

(5) _____ **Helps keep the discussion on track.**
    (Rating)

Meeting Date:_____ Critique:	Meeting Date:_____ Critique:	Meeting Date:_____ Critique:

Member _____ Critic _____
(One group member)   (Your name)

GROUP DYNAMICS PEER CRITIQUE FORM

Directions: Keep written documentation of the ethical group membership of each member in your group using the rating scale:

7	6	5	4	3	2	1
(Excellent)						(Poor)

(1) _____ **Committed to the goals of the group.**
(Rating)

Meeting Date: _____ Critique:	Meeting Date:_____ Critique:	Meeting Date:_____ Critique:

(2) _____ **Fulfills individual assignments.**
(Rating)

Meeting Date:_____ Critique:	Meeting Date:_____ Critique:	Meeting Date:_____ Critique:

234

(3) _____ **Avoids interpersonal conflicts.**
    (Rating)

Meeting Date:_____	Meeting Date:_____	Meeting Date:_____
Critique:	Critique:	Critique:

(4) _____ **Encourages group participation.**
    (Rating)

Meeting Date:_____	Meeting Date:_____	Meeting Date:_____
Critique:	Critique:	Critique:

(5) _____ **Helps keep the discussion on track.**
    (Rating)

Meeting Date:_____	Meeting Date:_____	Meeting Date:_____
Critique:	Critique:	Critique:

Name:_____Section:_____

SELF-CRITIQUE FORM:
THE ACTUATION PERSUASIVE SPEECH

Goal: To evaluate your own performance.

Rationale: As a form of cognitive restructuring, this exercise can help reduce public speaking anxiety while it helps you improve as a public speaker.

Directions: (a) In groups of 4 to 6 students, discuss your last speech performance based on the following guidelines. Then, complete and turn in this form based on your thoughts and the group discussion. OR (b) Watch a videotape of yourself giving your last speech. Complete this form and turn it in.

1. In terms of **Delivery,** the requirements for this speech were to sound intelligible, conversational, and express emotional conviction; and to look poised, wear appropriate attire, use effective eye contact, facial expression, gestures, motivated movement; and to convey initial and terminal ethos. I did the following things well in my last speech:

a.

b.

2. In terms of **Content,** the requirements were to be within the time constraint; offer ethos, pathos, and logos; round the cycle of learning, and offer depth, breadth and listener relevance; cite at least four external sources, and a clear call to action. I did the following things well in my last speech:

a.

b.

3. In terms of **Structure,** the requirements were to offer all macrostructural elements in a creative way, use clear, inclusive, colorful language, use persuasive "punch" words, use no slang or verbal garbage, and use style in connectives and phrasing. I did the following things well in my last speech:

a.

b.

4. In terms of my **PowerPoint Presentational Aids,** the requirements were to construct them well and integrate them effectively. I did the following things well in my last speech:

a.

b.

5. If I could do my last speech over again, I would do the following things differently:

a.

b.

c.

6. Overall, I would give myself a grade of _____ on my last speech because . . .

7. To improve as a public speaker on my next speech, I am going to try to:

a.

b.

SPECIAL OCCASION SPEECHES

SPEECH TO INTRODUCE A SPEAKER

Description: The major purpose of this speech should be to focus the audience on the featured speaker and create a desire for the audience to hear the speaker's message. Assume that you are introducing the featured speaker for some specific occasion. You should limit your remarks to areas that include why the speaker should be recognized, successes the speaker has experienced, qualities of the speaker that are laudable, and any additional points that contribute to the success of the speaker.

Special Requirements: If this were an actual introduction, the first thing that would be required of you would be to consult with the speaker prior to presenting the introduction. You must also analyze your audience to determine the length, language, and style of your speech. You must state the individual's name and the speech title. Your introduction should be brief but adequate, it should stress the importance of the speaker's subject, and it should be delivered with sincerity and enthusiasm. The suggested time limit is 1 to 2 minutes.

SPEECH OF PRESENTATION

Description: The purpose of this speech is to present an award, prize, or gift to an individual or group. It is also a way to formally recognize an accomplishment and share that information with the audience. Organize your presentation into three parts by showing what the award is for, by giving the criteria for winning or achieving the award, and by stating how the person won or achieved the award.

Special Requirements: Your remarks must include name and what the award is. You must present information that allows the audience to understand what the recipient has done and what criteria were met. For example, if you present an award for competition you must decide the type of contest, the number of contestants, and the way the contest was judged. Your presentation should be delivered with enthusiasm. The suggested time limit is 3–5 minutes.

SPEECH OF ACCEPTANCE

Description: You were presented an award and you need to accept it with gratitude in front of an audience.

Special Requirements: The ironic aspect about this speech is that it should not be about you. You should only thank the people who presented it to you and the people who helped you get it. Also, you should pay your respects to the other people who were up for the award. A third thing you should do is explain to the listeners what it took for you to win it.

SPEECH OF NOMINATION

Description: A speech of nomination reviews the accomplishments of an admired person and then nominates them for a position in a company or some other group.

Special Requirements: The important thing is that you don't say the name of the person until you finished listing their qualities. This could be helpful especially if the person is not well liked because the audience is more prone to listen.

SPEECH TO ENTERTAIN

Description: Your objective is to provide enjoyment for listeners. There are basically two approaches to this speech: Start with a ridiculous subject and deal with it in a mock serious tone; or select a serious subject and approach it with an exaggerated sense of humor. Your speech should accomplish three things: It should make a point; it should display an excellent use of language; and it should use strong emotional appeals. Topics should not offend anyone but rather allow us to laugh at each other. The humor of the speech will be attained in an area of supporting material. It is a good idea to employ a range of tactics as means of injecting humor into the speech. Finally, you must keep in mind at all times that you are giving a speech and that you must make a serious point.

Special Requirements: This speech should follow the same organizational format as the informative or persuasive speeches. Your speech needs to be energetic but also conversational and direct. You should avoid being overly dramatic. The suggested time limit is 5 minutes.

SPEECH OF TRIBUTE

Description: The goal with this speech is to praise a person's qualities or achievements. You will create a desire in your listeners to emulate the person or persons honored. Some types of tribute speeches include: farewells—when people retire or quit; dedications—commemorating a person, event, or occasion; eulogies—speeches at funerals.

Special Requirements: Other information that is included in speeches of tribute is discussing what qualities about the person should be carried on by other members of the company or why certain traditions should be carried on by the organization. The important thing is that the speaker **does not** itemize the accomplishments of the honored person or group because it weakens the impact.

SPEECH OF GOODWILL

Description: The speech of goodwill informs an audience about a product, service, operation, or procedure and it enhances the listeners' appreciation of a particular institution, practice, or profession. Some examples would include a luncheon meeting or a product show.

Special Requirements: The length of time that is spent on giving this speech depends on the content. If it is part of a larger banquet that is not based solely on this person, product, or service, the speech should be short and to the point, maybe lasting for 5 to 8 minutes. But if the meeting was arranged specifically for you to give this speech, it may last up to 30 minutes or more. All of the good qualities of a conversational and confident speaker should be present.

AWARD PRESENTATION ACTIVITY

Divide students into dyads. Each pair is given matching descriptions of a businessperson, entertainer, or celebrity and is asked to study the descriptions. One student in each dyad is asked to "present" the award and the other "accepts" it. The "accepting" student assumes the role of the individual in the description. Presuming students in the class are attending an awards banquet, the presenter and receiver prepare impromptu speeches for the occasion and deliver them in front of the group. Examples of fictitious awards might be "Entertainer of the Year," "Small Businessperson of the Year," etc., this role-playing activity helps students operationalize special occasion speeches and gain experience in impromptu speaking.

IMPROMPTU SPEECHES

OVERVIEW

The basic criteria for fulfilling the impromptu speaking assignment is explained in the syllabus. The objective of this type of speech is to provide you with an opportunity to demonstrate growth in poise and confidence when speaking before others without prior preparation. The following types of impromptu speeches may be assigned by your instructor.

SPEAKING ON A TOPIC

Description: Topics may be generated in a variety of ways. You and the rest of the students may be asked to bring ideas prior to the speaking day. The topics you select should be ones which are familiar and of interest to you. All students will have an equal chance to draw them. Each student will draw three topics and they must decide to speak on one of them. Or, the instructor may ask you to bring those topics on the speaking day and the instructor will select one of them. Then you will elaborate on two or three aspects of the topic for the listeners.

Special Requirements: Your remarks should be organized and follow a simple outline format which includes an introduction, a body with 2–3 main points, and a conclusion. You should try to include personal stories and observations to add interest to the speech. You should relate your experiences to the class. You may decide to describe why you agree or disagree with the topic or both. You will be expected to maintain a sense of poise and confidence. Deliver the speech in a conversational manner. The time limit is 2–3 minutes.

SPEAKING ON A QUOTATION

Description: One of the most common types of impromptu speeches is one that is focused on a quotation. Your instructor will find a sufficient amount of simple quotations from which you may draw from one quotation to three quotations from which to pick. Once you have chosen which one to speak on, you have about 2 minutes to prepare a speech.

Special Requirements: Again, your remarks should be organized and should follow a simple outline format which includes an introduction, a body with 2 to 3 main points, and a conclusion. You should try to include information on how you may have experienced the idea or how you wish to. Your speech should have all of the good qualities of a confident and conversational speaker. The time limit is 2 to 3 minutes.

IMPROMPTU SPEECHES

Rationale: This speech is designed to provide you an opportunity to organize and present your ideas about a topic with minimal preparation time. Although impromptu speeches take little time to prepare, much thought must go into them if a speaker is to "make sense" to his or her audience. After learning about and applying the aspects of effective public speaking (i.e., delivery, structure, and content) throughout the semester, students should be able to prepare and present a satisfactory impromptu speech for their classmates.

GRADING CRITERIA FOR THE IMPROMPTU SPEECH

- For this 10 point speech, you will earn a passing grade simply by attempting the performance. In other words, if you make a serious attempt to give this speech, you will earn **6 of the 10 points.** To earn additional points, you must demonstrate specific skills in terms of delivery, structure, and content.

Delivery

Use of Voice: If you can sound conversational (like you are talking with us rather than reading to us or presenting in front of us) and if you are intelligible, you will earn **1 additional point.**

Use of Body: If you can look poised and if you can demonstrate good eye contact and facial expressions, you will earn **1 additional point.**

Structure

If you offer an attention catcher, thesis statement, and preview in your introduction, transitions in your body, and a thesis restatement, summary and clincher in your conclusion, you will earn **1 additional point.**

Content

If you talk about two or three main points within the 2- to 3-minute time frame, you will earn **1 additional point.**

TIPS FOR IMPROMPTU SPEAKING

We do a lot of impromptu talking each day, but it is still the type of speech situation that many of us fear the most. What can we do to gain some control over the impromptu speaking situation? Read through the following tips:

1. Prepare for the unexpected times when you might be called upon to speak.

2. Be a careful listener as you can always incorporate previous speaker's remarks.

3. Don't panic when you are called upon. Use your time to organize your thoughts.

4. Formulate a central point around which you can build your comments.

5. Select only a few main points to elaborate on and select an appropriate pattern of organization.

6. Make the conclusion brief.

7. Don't ramble on and on and don't get off the subject.

8. Don't apologize at any point in the presentation! Your listeners don't expect an elaborate oration, so relax, be yourself, and enjoy the opportunity to share some of your thoughts with others.

IMPROMPTU SPEECH ORGANIZATION

Take a few moments after you are called upon to speak and organize your thoughts. Jot down your central point and your main points if you have the opportunity and follow this outline format:

Introduction: Attention-getting remarks
Listener Relevance Link
Thesis Statement
Preview Main Points

Body: (Try to limit your main points to 2 or 3.)

I. First Main Idea

A. Subpoint to develop the 1st idea.

B. Subpoint to develop the 1st idea.

II. Second Main Idea

A. Subpoint to develop the 2nd idea.

B. Subpoint to develop the 2nd idea.

Conclusion: Summarize your 2 to 3 main points
Thesis restatement
Clincher/Tie back to your attention catcher

IMPROMPTU SPEECH EXAMPLE

Formal Outline: "How Study Abroad Has Influenced My Life"

Anna Luebbering

Introduction

I. **Attention Catcher:** Meine sehrverehrten Damen und Herren, mein Name ist Anna Luebbering und bin in diesem Semester als Austauschschuelerin hier an der NDSU. Now you probably think: WHAT did she just say? Let me repeat the whole sentence in English. Ladies and Gentleman, my name is Anna Luebbering and I am a foreign exchange student here at NDSU for one semester.

II. **Listener Relevance:** Study abroad can be an important part of anyone's education.

III. **Thesis Statement:** Today I would like to talk about the influence abroad study has had on my life.

Body

I. **First Main Point:** I am originally from Germany, but I have studied in the Netherlands for the past 2 years.

   A. **Subpoint:** In the Netherlands, I study International Marketing Management at the International Business School in Groningen, a city in the north of the country.

   B. **Subpoint:** My curriculum requires one abroad study semester and one abroad internship semester. After having finished my first five semesters, it was time for me to go.

   Transition: When people learn about where I am from, they ask me why I chose to go to Fargo.

II. **Second Main Point:** In the school year of 1995/96, I was a foreign exchange student in Lamberton, a small town in southwestern Minnesota.

   A. **Subpoint:** This was my first abroad experience, which I really enjoyed. And I thought that the only chance to ever meet my American friends again would be to come back to study in the USA. And fortunately NDSU was the closest partner school in the USA.

   B. **Subpoint:** I now officially study Business Administration, but I am only taking one business class, two communication classes and one psychology class. I am also singing in the University Chorus.

   Transition: So, when I am done here, where am I going to go, and what am I going to do?

III. **Third Main Point:** My international experience is not over yet.

   A. **Subpoint:** When I return to Europe another interesting experience is waiting for me: my abroad internship. I do not have a placement so far but I am working on it.

   B. **Subpoint:** And I have another experience abroad planned for this summer. Some friends and I will go on vacation to Italy in a camper. Do I speak Italian? No. Does that keep me from going there? No!

C. **Subpoint:** My knowledge of at least one foreign language—English—has improved significantly, I have made a lot of interesting friends and I learned to appreciate cultures other than the one I grew up with.

Conclusion

I.   **Thesis restatement:** Today I have talked about the influence of an abroad study.

II. **Main point summary:** I told you where I usually study, how I got here and what I will do after this semester.

III. **Clincher:** Well, so far my abroad experience as a foreign exchange student as well as a student here at NDSU, have enriched my life in so many ways. Study abroad can enrich your life too. And maybe my speech today will encourage you to go for the abroad experience. Perhaps if you study in Europe, you will learn the meaning of: "Meine sehrvehrehrten Damen und Herren, mein Name ist Anna Luebbering und ich bin toll."

Name _____ Section _____

Topic _____

PREPARATION OUTLINE: IMPROMPTU SPEECH

Introduction

I.   **Attention Catcher:**

II. **Listener Relevance:**

III. **Speaker Credibility (optional):**

IV. **Thesis Statement:**

V.   **Preview:**

Body

I.   **First Main Point:**

   A. Subpoint

   B. Subpoint

   Transition:

II. **Second Main Point:**

   A. Subpoint

   B. Subpoint

Conclusion

I.   **Thesis restatement:**

II. **Main point summary:**

III. **Clincher:**

Name _____ Section _____

INSTRUCTOR CRITIQUE FORM: IMPROMPTU SPEECH

ASPECT	CRITIQUE
Delivery *Voice:* Conversational? Intelligible?	
Body: Eye Contact? Poise?	
Structure Attention Catcher? Thesis Statement? Preview? Transitions? Thesis Restatement? Summary of Main Points? Clincher?	
Content All main points addressed? Supporting material included? Met time constraint?	

Total Points: _____